D1555482

SAXON SERIES IN ENGLISH AS A SECOND LANGUAGE

GRANT TAYLOR, Consulting Editor

MODERN

SPOKEN

ENGLISH

AN ADVANCED PRACTICE BOOK

By THOMAS LEE CROWELL, Jr.
Late Professor of English,
Columbia University and Hunter College

McGRAW-HILL BOOK COMPANY

NEW YORK   LONDON   MEXICO CITY   SYDNEY   TORONTO

MODERN

Spoken

ENGLISH

1st Printing 1988

Copyright © 1961 by McGraw-Hill, Inc. All rights Reserved.
No part of this publication may be reproduced, stored in a
retrieval system, or transmitted, in any form or by any means,
electronic, mechanical, photocopying, recording, or otherwise,
without the prior written permission of the publisher.

The United States Library of Congress Catalog Card Number 61-15022

When ordering this title use ISBN 0-07-014730-2

Printed and bound in Singapore by B & JO Enterprise Pte Ltd.

SAXON SERIES IN ENGLISH AS A SECOND LANGUAGE

GRANT TAYLOR, Consulting Editor

ADVANCED ENGLISH EXERCISES

AMERICAN ENGLISH READER

AMERICAN READINGS

ENGLISH CONVERSATION PRACTICE

INDEX TO MODERN ENGLISH

LEARNING AMERICAN ENGLISH

MASTERING AMERICAN ENGLISH

MASTERING SPOKEN ENGLISH, Tapes 1

MASTERING SPOKEN ENGLISH, Records 1

MASTERING SPOKEN ENGLISH, Workbook 1

MODERN ENGLISH ESSAYS

MODERN ENGLISH WORKBOOK

MODERN SPOKEN ENGLISH

PRACTICING AMERICAN ENGLISH

READING AMERICAN HISTORY

McGRAW-HILL BOOK COMPANY

NEW YORK   LONDON   MEXICO CITY   SYDNEY   TORONTO

PREFACE

To the Student

Learning a language can be and should be enjoyable. It takes time and effort, though. It took you a long time and great effort to learn your first language. Your family and your friends patiently spent thousands of hours correcting and encouraging you when you were a child.

Learning a second language is both easier and harder than learning your first language was. It is easier because you can use your intelligence: you can consciously see patterns and fit new material into them. It is harder primarily because you have already established the habits of your first language and you have the tendency to follow those habits when you are learning a new language.

What's the best way to learn English? The answer is simple: practice. Can anybody learn English? If he has learned his first language, he can learn English.

This book provides you with a great deal of material for practice. It gives you directions about what to do to make the sounds of English. It is up to you to make those sounds. It is up to you to make the effort — to practice, practice, and practice — and practice correctly.

A language is made up of sounds. Those sounds make up words and sentences. All of those things are important, but the most important is the complete utterance. You should, of course, practice the sounds and the words, but your aim should be to master the complete utterance — to understand what is said to you in ordinary conversation and to be able to speak so that an English speaker can understand you.

The hundreds of sentences for practice that you will find in this book were selected for their naturalness. The words in those sentences appear in vocabulary lists based on frequency in oral and written English, such as *A General Service List of English Words* by

Michael West and *The Words and Sounds of Telephone Conversations* by N. R. French, C. W. Carter, Jr., and Walter Koening, Jr. Those words are in sentences that you will encounter in conversation. You will hear educated persons use them, and you will need them to converse with educated persons.

Possibly the most valuable part of the book is the dialogs. They are English in context. You should memorize them, paying close attention to pronunciation, phrasing, stress, and intonation. Repeat them over and over again. Practice them with a friend, each of you taking alternate lines. Study the sentences until you can say them without stopping and without looking at the words.

I hope you will enjoy using *Modern Spoken English*.

To the Teacher

Intonation begins this book. A dozen years of experience in teaching students to improve their speech have shown that the basic feature that must be assimilated is intonation. The explanation of intonation has intentionally been kept simple: only three general patterns are discussed. However, from the very first class to the very last class you should drill, drill, drill the students on those patterns. Intonation is the frame of speech; if the frame is wrong, the words will be unintelligible.

Inseparable from intonation is stress: word stress, group or phrase stress, and sentence stress. Again, the discussion of that aspect of speech is brief, but realization of its importance is crucial in mastering the spoken language. Virtually all students are overly syllable-oriented: they tend to pronounce each syllable with emphasis and without regard to its relation to the other parts of the utterance. To combat that tendency, this book has a wealth of exercises on word stress, group stress, and sentence stress. You should insist on all three facets of stress: length, pitch, and volume; but of those three, length is undoubtedly the most important for pedagogic purposes. Most of your students are likely unaware of the role that difference in length plays in stressed and unstressed syllables; making them conscious of it and expert with it will bring satisfying results.

Contractions such as *'s* for *has* or *is* and *'ll* for *will* or *shall* are the products of the English speaker's habit of reducing unstressed syllables. Some students have been told that contractions are inelegant. You should reassure those students: contractions are customary in cultivated speech. It is true that the full forms such as *is* and *will* are usual in writing, and it is probably wise for students to write the full forms; however, they must learn to use the contractions if they want to speak naturally, and they must learn to comprehend them since they will hear them constantly.

Possibly the most radical departure from books with a similar purpose is in the treatment of articulation. Precise directions for physically producing each sound of English with the speech mechanism are given. Some of them may differ from your own manner of articulation, but I recommend that a student be taught to follow all of them for one practical reason: they have been proved to be effective.

A frequent complaint of teachers is that books do not contain enough material for class drill. A constant complaint of students is that they do not have enough material for practice outside of class. This book has been prepared to provide both kinds of material. Each topic for concentration has numerous illustrative sentences which can be used immediately in class and assigned for practice at home and for review repetition in a later class period. In addition, once a topic has been introduced, there are usually subsequent sections devoted to review of it. In that way, a large number of topics are covered rapidly, but the necessary drill and review are not neglected.

The dialogs have been composed carefully to give students practice in the kind of speech they will most often need: quick exchange between two persons. The words and patterns are those of standard conversation: they are not slang or vulgar. I suggest that they be used in the following manner: you say the four or five sentences of the dialog with a conversational delivery. Then, repeat each sentence, and either you or a student point out the intonation, the stressed syllables, and the places where pauses are obligatory or optional. Then, have two students say the lines alternately as a conversation; then, two different students; etc. Tell the students to practice the dialog outside of class, and then in the next class meeting have pairs of students repeat the dialog without looking at the book.

Proverbs, epigrams, excerpts from poetry and prose — "familiar quotations" are part of the stock of a language. They constantly crop up in speech and writing. They have a deep semantic content and are expressions of the general culture of a language group. Some have become hackneyed through unthinking repetition, but their very triteness is significant. To know a language thoroughly, a person must know its familiar sayings. The selections in this book are representative: they have been chosen to give students a taste of the wide variety in English. Those which have a figurative meaning are usually easily interpreted by students, but you as a teacher are aware of the fact that that which is obvious to some persons may not be clear to others; you may have to explicate some of the quotations. Some of the lines are humorous — for example, the tongue twisters and the extracts from Lewis Carroll. Their intent will be plain to some students but not to all. As you know, the humor of a language is customarily the most difficult aspect to be learned. Nevertheless, it should not be avoided; students should be exposed to it as soon as possible; they will soon come to appreciate and enjoy it. A quotation should be gone over in class thoroughly, with the pronunciation, intonation, and phrasing clearly established. However, do not forget to make sure that all the students understand the meaning. Then, have the students memorize the quotation and repeat it at the next meeting without looking at their books.

Have the students write. Writing reinforces speaking. Writing is the visualization of speech. Accuracy in reproduction is the goal you are helping your students attain; accurate copying is a simple but valuable aid toward that goal. I have my students copy and hand in as homework all the sentences, dialogs, and quotations gone over in the previous meeting.

Dictation is invaluable. It often reveals sources of difficulty: a student, for instance, may not have come to realize that the articles *a, an,* and *the* are meaningful sounds; he may think that they are only concomitant noises. Similarly, other students may not be alert to the sounds of inflections. Practice in memorizing and taking of dictation will lead students to associate the sounds with their written representations. I use dictation to a great extent. I tell students in advance to be prepared to write from dictation any of the sentences, dialogs, or quotations gone over previously. Then, in every meeting of the class, I dictate five or so sentences exactly as they appear in the book. I select a few sentences from early as well as recent lessons in order to goad students into reviewing constantly. Most important, I say each sentence *only once*. I do not repeat. At first, the students find the procedure extremely difficult, but in time they come to be quite expert. You must be patient but also inflexible: you must resist the pleas of the students to repeat the sentence.

Here is a final word on the phonetic symbols. Since English spelling is not phonetic, a person learning the language profits from having a device for clearly seeing that there are differences or similarities between the sounds of certain words. If he is shown graphically that there are differences, he will try to hear the differences. He will also realize that although certain sounds are spelled differently — for example, the vocalic in *sir, word,* and *earn* — they are pronounced the same. Many different phonetic-symbol systems are in use, and many teachers compose their own systems or variations of existing systems. I adhere fairly closely to the system established by the International Phonetic Association. One cogent reason is that the system serves my own purposes adequately. For instance, I have learned that it is pedagogically more effective not to teach that the difference between closely related vowels, such as [i] and [ɪ], is solely a matter of length. For most students the difference between tenseness and laxness is more relevant. Separate symbols visualize that difference. The same is true of triplets such as [s] and [ʃ] and [tʃ].

Here I would like to give you a word of advice: phonetic symbols should not become an end in themselves, at least not for students who are striving to learn to speak the language. I find that little work needs to be done directly with or on phonetic symbols; students should be able to recognize them and understand that a different symbol means a different sound. Too great an emphasis on the symbols will have a natural result: students will begin to write English phonetically, and doing so, no matter how we may feel about it, is socially unacceptable.

I hope you will enjoy teaching *Modern Spoken English.*

T. L. C.

New York City
1961

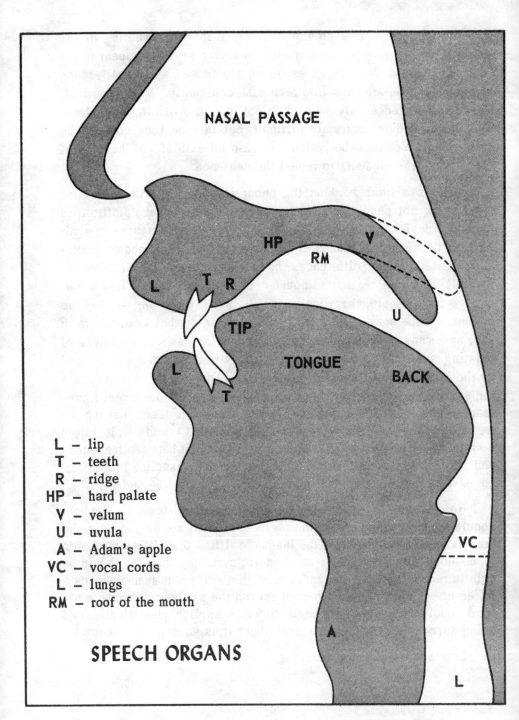

NASAL PASSAGE

HP

RM

V

L T R

TIP

U

L

T

TONGUE

BACK

L – lip
T – teeth
R – ridge
HP – hard palate
V – velum
U – uvula
A – Adam's apple
VC – vocal cords
L – lungs
RM – roof of the mouth

VC

A

L

SPEECH ORGANS

CONTENTS

LESSON 1   Intonation

Intonation is the rising and falling of the pitch of your voice as you speak.

It is very important for you to realize that native speakers react to intonation. If you use the wrong kind, your listener may misinterpret your intention. He will certainly be confused, and he may even be insulted.

Your intonation, for example, can signify that you are making a statement or that you are asking a question or that you have not finished speaking.

I suggest that you follow three general rules in your intonation:

1. Let your voice fall to its lowest pitch at the end of statements and at the end of questions beginning with the *"wh words"* *who, whose, whom, which, what, when, where, why,* and *how.*

I'm tired.	Where's my notebook?
It's blue.	When are you leaving?
She's Spanish.	What do you think of him?
That's all right.	Who went with you?
Come back tomorrow.	How did you know that?
Say it again.	Why don't you tell me?

2. Let your voice rise to a high pitch at the end of a question which does not begin with one of the *wh* words.

Has he gone?	Is it raining?
Do you like it?	It's blue?
Did you lose your book?	I can't go?
Does that look all right?	Going home now?
Are you sure?	Anything else?

3. Let your voice stay on a middle pitch if you pause before you have finished a sentence.

I bought a table ... a chair ... and a bookcase.
We don't need them ... but they look nice.
I'll return them ... if you want me to.
We can do without them ... or wait a while longer.

Whenever you practice sentences in this book, follow the three intonation patterns.

1

EXERCISE 1 Practice the following, applying the principles previously discussed.

1. What's the matter?
2. I'm tired.
3. What've you been doing?
4. I've been working.
5. Have you?
6. All day long.
7. Where did you work?
8. In the office.
9. Who else was there?
10. My secretary.
11. Is she Spanish?
12. Yes, she is.
13. Going home now?
14. In a few minutes.
15. You can't go.
16. I can't go?
17. It's raining.
18. Are you sure?
19. Look out the window.
20. Oh, that's too bad.
21. What're you going to do?
22. I'll wait a while longer.

LESSON 2 Silent Letters

As you know, you can not always tell how to pronounce an English word from its spelling. Sometimes the same letter represents different sounds — for example, *u* in *busy, bury, pull, sun,* and *rude.* Sometimes a letter represents no sound: it is "silent" or not pronounced. Many common words contain silent letters. Some of them are the following:

b in *debt, doubt,* and *subtle.*

d in *Wednesday* (the first *d).*

gh in *though, thorough,* and *through.*

h in *Thai, John, Thomas, Thames, Esther* and in *hour, honor, heir* and their derivatives such as *hourly, honorable, honest, dishonest,* and *heiress.*

i in *business, fruit, juice, suit,* and *bruise.*

l in *could, should, would,* and *Lincoln* (the second *l).*

p in *receipt* and *corps.*

s in *corps, aisle,* and *island.*

t in *Christmas.*

u in *build, buy, guard, guess, guest, guide, guilt, guitar,* and *liquor.*

w in *answer, sword, two, who, whose, whom, whole,* and *wholly.*

2

EXERCISE 2 Practice the following, applying the principles previously discussed.

1. John joined the air corps last Wednesday.
2. He won't need his business suits any more.
3. He wasn't thoroughly honorable.
4. I wouldn't say he was dishonest.
5. Fruit juice didn't suit him.
6. He got in debt through buying liquor.
7. There was no doubt about his guilt.
8. He'd signed a receipt for two cases.
9. He should have married an heiress.

LESSON 3 Phonetic Symbols

Because English does not have phonetic spelling, it is helpful to have a system for indicating the sounds of words. Such a system is called a "phonetic alphabet." In the following alphabet, each symbol represents one distinctive English sound, and each distinctive English sound is represented by one symbol. The brackets [ ] indicate that the writing inside is in phonetic symbols, not in the ordinary English letters. The stress mark ['] is placed before the stressed syllable of a word.

CONSONANTS

Voiceless (produced without vibration of the vocal cords)

1. [p] as in *pipe* [paɪp], *pity* ['pɪtɪ], *happy* ['hæpɪ], *lips* [lɪps]

2. [t] as in *tea* [ti], *tight* [taɪt], *too* [tu], *letter* ['lɛtə] *states* [stets]

3. [k] as in *cake* [kek], *custom* ['kəstəm], *like* [laɪk], *question* ['kwɛstʃən], *rocks* [rɑks]

4. [f] as in *find* [faɪnd], *full* [fʊl], *half* [hæf], *life* [laɪf], *coughs* [kɔfs]

5. [θ] as in *think* [θɪŋk], *breath* [brɛθ], *nothing* ['nəθɪŋ]

6. [s] as in *say* [se], *city* ['sɪtɪ], *miss* [mɪs], *last* [læst], *hits* [hɪts], *kisses* ['kɪsɪz]

3

7. [ʃ]   as in *ship* [ʃɪp], *dish* [dɪʃ], *machine* [məˈʃin],
          crashes [ˈkræʃɪz]

8. [tʃ]   as in *cheap* [tʃip], *church* [tʃətʃ], *match* [mætʃ],
          catches [ˈkætʃɪz]

9. [h]   as in *how* [haʊ], *hot* [hɑt], *ahead* [əˈhɛd]

Voiced   (produced with vibration of the vocal cords)

10. [b]   as in *baby* [ˈbebɪ], *tub* [təb], *robber* [ˈrɑbə],
          rubs [rəbz]

11. [d]   as in *dead* [dɛd], *did* [dɪd], *mad* [mæd], *lady* [ˈledɪ],
          needs [nidz]

12. [g]   as in *go* [go], *bag* [bæg], *beggar* [ˈbɛgə], *legs* [lɛgz]

13. [v]   as in *voice* [vɔɪs], *heaven* [ˈhɛvən], *save* [sev],
          shaves [ʃevz]

14. [ð]   as in *this* [ðɪs], *breathe* [brið], *father* [fɑðə]

15. [z]   as in *zoo* [zu], *rose* [roz], *days* [dez], *quizzes* [ˈkwɪzɪz]

16. [ʒ]   as in *vision* [ˈvɪʒən], *pleasure* [ˈplɛʒə]

17. [dʒ] as in *judge* [dʒədʒ], *age* [edʒ], *edges* [ˈɛdʒɪz]

18. [l]   as in *late* [let], *cold* [kold], *silly* [ˈsɪlɪ], *hills* [hɪlz]

19. [r]   as in *red* [rɛd], *far* [fɑr], *sorry* [ˈsɑrɪ], *cars* [kɑrz]

20. [j]   as in *yet* [jɛt], *union* [ˈjunjən], *acute* [əˈkjut]

21. [w]   as in *wait* [wet], *away* [əˈwe], *white* [hwaɪt]

22. [m]   as in *make* [mek], *bomb* [bɑm], *homes* [homz]

23. [n]   as in *nine* [naɪn], *manner* [ˈmænə], *know* [no],
          pans [pænz]

24. [ŋ]   as in *thing* [θɪŋ], *angry* [ˈæŋgrɪ], *thank* [θæŋk],
          sings [sɪŋz]

VOWELS

1. [i]   as in *see* [si], *each* [itʃ], *key* [ki], *leisure* ['liʒə],
         scene [sin], *chief* [tʃif], *machine* [mə'ʃin],
         peas [piz], *freed* [frid]

2. [ɪ]   as in *sit* [sɪt], *Monday* ['məndɪ], *fear* [fɪr],
         weird [wɪrd], *been* [bɪn], *busy* ['bɪzɪ],
         cottage ['katɪdʒ], *England* ['ɪŋglənd],
         marriage ['mærɪdʒ], *sieve* [sɪv], *build* [bɪld],
         myth [mɪθ], *women* ['wɪmɪn]

3. [e]   as in *take* [tek], *fail* [fel], *say* [se], *break* [brek],
         gauge [gedʒ], *they* [ðe], *neighbor* ['nebə]

4. [ɛ]   as in *set* [sɛt], *bread* [brɛd], *many* ['mɛnɪ], *said* [sɛd],
         friend [frɛnd], *guess* [gɛs], *leopard* ['lɛpəd],
         bury ['bɛrɪ]

5. [æ]   as in *sat* [sæt], *laugh* [læf], *plaid* [plæd]

6. [ə]   as in *sun* [sən], *son* [sən], *flood* [fləd], *rough* [rəf],
         alone [ə'lon], *apartment* [ə'partmənt],
         specimen ['spɛsəmən], *gallop* ['gæləp],
         Plymouth ['plɪməθ], *jealous* ['dʒɛləs],
         campus ['kæmpəs]

7. [a]   as in *top* [tap], *calm* [kam], *heart* [hart]

8. [ɔ]   as in *law* [lɔ], *call* [kɔl], *haul* [hɔl], *cost* [kɔst],
         broad [brɔd], *ought* [ɔt]

9. [o]   as in *low* [lo], *note* [not], *coal* [kol], *toe* [to],
         sew [so], *soul* [sol]

10. [ʊ] as in *pull* [pʊl], *took* [tʊk], *wolf* [wʊlf], *would* [wʊd]

11. [u] as in *pool* [pul], *group* [grup], *lose* [luz], *shoe* [ʃu],
         rude [rud], *threw* [θru], *glue* [glu], *fruit* [frut]

12. [ə]   as in *term* [təm], *first* [fəst], *word* [wəd], *turn* [tən],
                heard [həd], *journey* ['dʒənɪ], *permit* [pə'mɪt],
                similar ['sɪmələ], *actor* ['æktə], *surpass* [sə'pæs]

DIPHTHONGS

1. [aɪ]   as in *mine* [maɪn], *cry* [kraɪ], *lie* [laɪ], *height* [haɪt],
            buy [baɪ]

2. [aʊ]   as in *loud* [laʊd], *how* [haʊ]

3. [ɔɪ]   as in *oil* [ɔɪl], *boy* [bɔɪ]

All vowels and diphthongs are voiced — that is, produced with vibration of the vocal cords.

EXERCISE 3 Practice the following, applying the principles previously discussed.

The English Alphabet in Phonetic Symbols

a	[e]	h	[etʃ]	o	[o]	v	[vi]
b	[bi]	i	[aɪ]	p	[pi]	w	['dəbljʊ]
c	[si]	j	[dʒe]	q	[kju]	x	[ɛks]
d	[di]	k	[ke]	r	[ar]	y	[waɪ]
e	[i]	l	[ɛl]	s	[ɛs]	z	[zi] *American*
f	[ɛf]	m	[ɛm]	t	[ti]	z	[zɛd] *British*
g	[dʒi]	n	[ɛn]	u	[ju]		

REVIEW: DIALOGS 1-5

1. 1 – Today's the first day of school.
    2 – Yes, it is.
    1 – Aren't you glad?
    2 – I don't know.

2. 1 – Did it take you long to get registered?
    2 – It certainly did.
    1 – What did you have to do?
    2 – Take tests, fill out forms, and wait.

REVIEW: DIALOGS (Continued)

3. 1 — It's very warm today.
   2 — Yes, it is.
   1 — It'll probably rain soon.
   2 — Yes, it probably will.

4. 1 — I went to a movie last night.
   2 — Did you like it?
   1 — Yes, very much.
   2 — What was it about?
   1 — Love, of course.

5. 1 — The weather's nice today.
   2 — Yes, it is.
   1 — We need rain, though.
   2 — Yes, we do.

REVIEW: QUOTATIONS 1-5

1. A thing of beauty is a joy forever.
   — *Keats*

2. All's well that ends well.
   — *Shakespeare*

3. The sea! the sea! the open sea!
   The blue, the fresh, the ever free.
   — *Cornwall*

4. A little nonsense now and then
   Is relished by the wisest men.
   — *Anonymous*

5. Every day, in every way,
   I am getting better and better.
   — *Coué*

LESSON 4 Stress: Words

Every English word of more than one syllable has at least one stressed syllable. A stressed syllable is pronounced in such a way that it is more prominent than an unstressed syllable. We stress a syllable by "saying it louder"; that is, we usually utter it with more

7

volume of breath and with a higher pitch than we do the surrounding syllables.

Vowels in stressed syllables are usually "longer" than vowels in unstressed syllables. The lengthening is usually made by "gliding off" the vowel, that is, by adding a sound to the vowel. Add an unemphatic [ɪ] after the "front" vowels [i], [ɪ], [e], [ɛ], and [æ]. Add an [ə] after the "back" vowels [u], [ʊ], [o], [ɔ], and [ɑ].

Sometimes a word has a secondary stress. We pronounce the syllable that bears a secondary stress with a little less volume and lower pitch than the syllable with the primary stress, and we do not say it as long.

Syllables which are not stressed are pronounced with relatively little breath. Most important, the vowel in an unstressed syllable is usually [ə] or [ɪ]. There are no easy rules for determining whether [ə] or [ɪ] should be used in the unstressed syllable. To be positive, you should consult a good dictionary. A very reliable guide is Kenyon and Knott's *Pronouncing Dictionary of American English.*

Since one of the characteristics of a "foreign accent" is stressing or pronouncing an unstressed syllable clearly, my advice is this: Don't worry about whether the unstressed vowel is [ə] or [ɪ]; use either and with relatively little clarity. Your concern should be about stressing the proper syllable and about *not* stressing unstressed syllables.

A useful device for learning to distinguish stress is "tapping." Take a pencil, and knock the end of it lightly on a table or chair for an unstressed syllable, and knock it more forcefully for a stressed syllable. For example, when you say the word *people,* strike once forcefully and once lightly. For the word *believe,* strike once lightly and once forcefully. For *returning,* strike once lightly, once forcefully, and once lightly. For *comfortable,* strike once forcefully and three times lightly. Give more time to the vowels in the stressed syllables than to those in the unstressed syllables

The place of stress in certain words seems to be particularly troublesome for some of you. Here are some of those words with the stressed vowel underlined. Say that vowel louder, longer, and higher.

admirable	character	democracy	italics	probably
afraid	comfortable	develop	machine	register
apostrophe	comparable	development	mistake	responsible
appetite	congress	distribute	obstacle	result
Arabic	constantly	effort	origin	theater
catastrophe	contribute	horizon	politics	vegetable
Catholic	degree	image	preface	

EXERCISE 4 Practice the following, applying the principles previously discussed.

1. What's the origin of character?
2. Does worry contribute to its development?
3. My sister worries about catastrophes.
4. She's never comfortable.
5. She sees all kinds of obstacles.
6. I feel responsible to some degree.
7. Politics constantly bothers her.
8. In her opinion, all voters should register.
9. She's afraid Congress may make a mistake.
10. It would be the result of no effort.
11. My sister's really an admirable woman.
12. She's the image of her mother.

LESSON 5 Production of Sounds

In the production of English sounds, these things are important: your breath, your vocal cords, the roof of your mouth, your tongue, your tooth ridge, your teeth, your lips, and your nose. With the exception of your breath, those things are called your *speech organs*. See the illustration of the speech organs at the beginning of this book.

Your *breath* is moved from your lungs out either through your mouth or through your nose. If a sound is made by your mouth, it is called an "oral" sound. If it is made through your nose, it is called a "nasal" sound.

Your *vocal cords* are in the hard, angular piece of bone that sticks out of your throat. It moves up and down when you swallow. You can feel it with your fingers. If the vocal cords vibrate when you make a sound, that sound is "voiced." If the cords do not vibrate, the sound is "voiceless." You can feel the vibration when you say a sound like [ɑ] in *father* or the [m] in *my*.

LESSON 5 (Continued)

The *roof* of your mouth is your *palate*. Feel it with your tongue. The front part is hard, and the back part is soft. Your *velum* is the soft back part of the roof. The part that hangs down in the back of your throat is called the *uvula*. You can see it in a mirror. When you make an oral sound, the velum is raised so that your breath can not go up into your nose. When you make a nasal sound, the velum is lowered so that your breath can be expelled through your nose.

Your *tongue* is very active when you speak. You can raise it, lower it, move it front, and move it back.

Your *tooth ridge* is the hard projection above and behind your upper teeth. (You have a tooth ridge for your lower teeth, but that is not very important in the production of sounds.) Put your tongue on the back of your upper front teeth, and then move it upward. Right above the teeth you will feel the ridge. Continue to move your tongue upward. It will suddenly go straight upward: it has left the tooth ridge.

Your *teeth* are important because you form English sounds by putting your tongue or your lower lip near the teeth. In producing some sounds of your native language, you probably touch the back of your upper teeth with your tongue, but you should take care not to do so for English sounds.

You make a number of sounds by either closing your *lips* or putting them into varied positions.

LESSON 6 Vowels: Tongue Position

The position of the tongue in the mouth is very important in the production of the vowels. You can move your tongue "front" — that is, toward your lips. You can move it "back" — that is, towards your throat. You can move it "high" — that is, toward the roof of your mouth. You can move it "low" — that is, towards the bottom of your mouth.

These vowels are **front vowels**: [i], [ɪ], [e], [ɛ], and [æ].

These vowels are **back vowels**: [u], [ʊ], [o], [ɔ], and [ɑ].

To feel the movement of your tongue, say *feed* [fid] and then say *food* [fud].

These vowels are **high vowels**: [i], [ɪ], [u], and [ʊ].

These vowels are **low vowels**: [æ], and [ɑ].

10

To feel the movement of your tongue, say *seed* [sid], then *sad* [sæd], then *sod* [sɑd], and then *sued* [sud]. As you say those words, feel your tongue move from "high front" for *seed,* to "low front" for *sad,* to "low back" for *sod,* and to "high back" for *sued.* Also notice that your lower jaw moves down when you go from "high" to "low," and that it moves up when you go from "low" to "high."

Between the high front vowels and the low front vowel there are the "mid front" vowels [e] and [ɛ], as in *main* [men] and *men* [mɛn].

Between the high back vowels and the low back vowel there are the "mid back" vowels [o] and [ɔ], as in *so* [so] and *saw* [sɔ].

EXERCISE 5 Say the words in the following list. Your tongue gradually moves from high front to low front to low back to high back. Notice also that your lower jaw gradually goes down and then up. Your lips become more and more open as you progress from the high vowels to the low vowels. With the back vowels, your lips become more and more round as you progress from low to high.

[i]	peel	[pil]	feel	[fil]
[ɪ]	pill	[pɪl]	fill	[fɪl]
[e]	pale	[pel]	fail	[fel]
[ɛ]	pell	[pɛl]	fell	[fɛl]
[æ]	pal	[pæl]	fallow	['fælo]
[ɑ]	Poll	[pɑl]	follow	['fɑlo]
[ɔ]	Paul	[pɔl]	fall	[fɔl]
[o]	pole	[pol]	foal	[fol]
[ʊ]	pull	[pʊl]	full	[fʊl]
[u]	pool	[pul]	fool	[ful]

REVIEW: DIALOGS 6-10

6. 1 – Do you think English is easy?
   2 – No, I don't.
   1 – Why not?
   2 – I have to work too hard.

7. 1 – That's a nice-looking hat you have on.
   2 – Thank you.
   1 – Where did you get it?
   2 – At Macy's.

REVIEW: DIALOGS (Continued)

8. 1 – Have you done your homework?
   2 – No, I haven't.
   1 – Why not?
   2 – I didn't have time last night.
   1 – That's no excuse.

9. 1 – Are you coming to school tomorrow if it rains?
   2 – Of course.
   1 – Aren't you afraid of getting wet?
   2 – Of course not.

10. 1 – It was very windy yesterday.
    2 – Yes, it was.
    1 – It's all clear today, though.
    2 – Yes, it is.

REVIEW: QUOTATIONS 6-9

6. The day is cold and dark and dreary;
   It rains, and the wind is never weary.

   – Longfellow

7. If at first you don't succeed,
   Try, try again.

   – Hickson

8. Rain, rain, go away.
   Come again another day.

   – Howell

9. The world is so full of a number of things,
   I'm sure we should all be as happy as kings.

   – Stevenson

LESSON 7   The Vowels: Tense and Lax

Most of you have trouble distinguishing pairs of English vowels such as [i] and [ɪ], as in *feel* and *fill*. It may help you to know that you can feel the difference between such pairs.

Some vowels are "tense" — that is, the muscles in the speech organs are relatively "tight" or tense when those sounds are made.

12

You can feel the tenseness in your tongue and in the muscles along the lower part of your face. The tense vowels are [i], [e], [æ], [ɑ], [o], and [u].

The most relaxed vowel is [ə]. Your speech organs are in a neutral position; your tongue sits down, and it's not tense at all; your lips are relaxed, your lower jaw is in a middle position – it's not "pulled" either up or down.

The low vowels [æ] and [ɑ] are both tense. For [æ], press the tip of your tongue against the gum below your lower front teeth. Keep the rest of the tongue as flat as you can. For [ɑ], pull your tongue back and down as far as you comfortably can. Now, as a contrast to those two low vowels, you can use [ə]. For [ə], be as relaxed as you can. Let your tongue sit down. If you feel any tightness, you won't make the sound correctly.

EXERCISE 6 Pronounce the following pairs. The vowel in the first word of the pair is tense, and the vowel in the second word is lax.

[i]	–	[ɪ]		[u]	–	[ʊ]
feet		fit		shoed		should
seat		sit		wooed		would
sheep		ship		cooed		could
beat		bit		fool		full
leak		lick		pool		pull

[e]	–	[ɛ]		[o]	–	[ɔ]
age		edge		low		law
late		let		so		saw
date		debt		coat		caught
mate		met		woke		walk
taste		test		boat		bought

EXERCISE 7 Pronounce the following triplets. For [æ] and [ɑ], make your tongue tense; for [ə], relax.

[æ]	[ə]	[ɑ]
backs	bucks	box
cap	cup	cop
cat	cut	cot
hat	hut	hot
lack	luck	lock

EXERCISE 8 Practice the following, applying the principles previously discussed.

1. My shoes don't fit my feet.
2. That ship is full of sheep.
3. Cats will lick a water leak.
4. If he would woo her, he would win her.
5. A fool is full of nonsense.
6. My age puts me on edge.
7. He paid the debt on the right date.
8. You test a pie by its taste.
9. If you saw it, it must be so.
10. He went for a walk after he woke.
11. The horse backs and bucks when he sees a box.
12. The cat cut its foot on the cot.
13. It's just my luck to lack a lock for the door.
14. Please sit in that seat.
15. My dog bit me when I beat him.
16. He shoed the horse when he should.
17. The pigeon cooed as loud as it could.
18. Let's pull him out of the pool.
19. Don't let yourself be late.
20. The captain met the mate on the bridge.
21. It's against the law to fly low.
22. He caught his coat on a nail.
23. She bought a boat for her son.
24. The beggar put his cap over his cup when he saw a cop.
25. He took off his hat in the hot hut.

LESSON 8   Diphthongs

The diphthongs are made by starting with the vowel in the first part of the diphthong and then moving the tongue. For [aɪ], put your tongue in the position for [ɑ] and then quickly raise it toward the front of your mouth. For [au], move your tongue from [ɑ] upward and make your lips round. For [ɔɪ], raise your tongue from [ɔ] toward the front of your mouth.

[aɪ]	[au]	[ɔɪ]
buy	bough	boy
sigh	sow	soy
vied	vowed	void

14

EXERCISE 9 Practice the following, applying the principles previously discussed.

1. I want to buy some cigarets.
2. A female hog is called a sow.
3. Electra vowed to revenge her father.
4. Outer space is not a void.
5. She sighed because she was tired.
6. The wind moved the boughs of the tree.
7. The boys vied with each other to win the prize.
8. Some plastics are made from soy beans.

LESSON 9 Two-Syllable Words: Stress on First Syllable

The following words have stress on the first syllable. When you pronounce them, be sure to lengthen the stressed vowel.

1. [i]   chiefly, creature, eager
2. [ɪ]   bitter, building, business, busy, cheerful, chicken, chimney, Christmas, women
3. [e]   able, agent, ancient, baby, basin
4. [ɛ]   airplane, any, beggar, berry, better, blessing, breakfast, bury, careful, careless
5. [æ]   absence, absent, action, active, actor, actress, after, angle
6. [ə]   brother, bucket, bundle, butter, button, color
7. [ɑ]   argue, armor, army, artist, barber, bargain, body
8. [ɔ]   also, always, August
9. [o]   cocoa, golden, holy
10. [ʊ]   cushion, woman
11. [u]   beauty, cruel, doing
12. [ɚ]   certain, courage, current
13. [aɪ]   brighten, childhood, dying
14. [aʊ]   mountain
15. [ɔɪ]   noisy

EXERCISE 10 Practice the following, applying the principles previously discussed.

1. Do you like berries for breakfast?
2. The agent was able to sell the building.
3. You got a bargain for your money.
4. It takes courage to climb a high mountain.

EXERCISE 10 (Continued)

5. I don't like to be cruel to any creature.
6. Artists like the golden light of August.
7. He was chiefly responsible.
8. Absence makes the heart grow fonder.
9. Children are active, eager, and noisy.
10. Don't argue with a barber.
11. The actor sat on the cushion and played with the baby.
12. The beggar carried a bundle of old clothes.

REVIEW: DIALOGS 11-15

11. 1 – This is my new car.
    What do you think of it?
    2 – It's a good-looking car.
    I'll bet it's fast.
    1 – It certainly is.

12. 1 – Excuse me.
    Are you Mr. Taylor?
    2 – No, I'm not.
    That's Mr. Taylor over there.
    The tall fellow with the brown hair.
    1 – Oh, yes.
    I see him now.

13. 1 – Have you ever worked here before?
    2 – No, I never have.
    1 – Have you ever been here?
    2 – Yes, I have.
    Twice before.

14. 1 – How much is the fare to Detroit?
    2 – Eighty dollars one way.
    A hundred fifty round trip.
    1 – I'll take a round-trip ticket, please.
    2 – All right.

REVIEW: DIALOGS (Continued)

15. 1— When can the director see me?
    2— Probably this afternoon.
       Can you come at two o'clock?
    1— No, I can't, but I can at three.
    2— All right. He'll be waiting.

REVIEW: QUOTATIONS 10-13

10. Into each life some rain must fall;
    Some days must be dark and dreary.
    — *Longfellow*

11. Hear the sledges with the bells — silver bells —
    What a world of merriment their melody foretells.
    — *Poe*

12. Set all things in their own peculiar place,
    And know that order is the greatest grace.
    — *Dryden*

13. Early to bed and early to rise
    Makes a man healthy, wealthy, and wise.
    — *Franklin*

LESSON 10   Group Stress: Articles

Certain kinds of words are usually stressed in sentences, and other kinds of words are usually not stressed.

In general, these kinds of words are stressed: nouns, main verbs, adjectives, adverbs, the demonstratives *this, that, these,* and *those,* and the *wh* words *who, whose, whom, which, what, when, where, why,* and *how.*

The kinds of words which are usually not stressed are these: the articles, possessive adjectives, prepositions, conjunctions, personal pronouns, the verb *be,* and auxiliary verbs.

The articles *a, an,* and *the* are usually not stressed. Think of them as being an unstressed part of the next word. Say *a man* as if the two words were written together: *aman.* In the same way, say *the boy* like one word. Don't stop between the two words.

The article *an* should also be thought of as part of the next word. However, don't "carry over" the [n] to the following vowel: stop the breath from coming out of the nose before you begin pronouncing the following vowel.

EXERCISE 11 Before each of the words in the following list (they are all nouns), add, first, the article *a* and, then, the article *the;* for instance, *a book* and *the book*. Be sure to lengthen the stressed vowel in the nouns. Exaggerate that vowel by saying it longer and louder and by gliding off it with an [ɪ] or [ə] sound. For example, say [əbʊ‿ə‿k].

book	heart	mind	sun	color	present
case	home	month	thing	country	question
cause	horse	part	voice	father	reason
chance	king	plan	war	figure	second
change	land	plant	watch	garden	story
course	laugh	play	wife	husband	system
day	law	point	wish	lady	table
door	life	price	word	letter	woman
dress	line	rest	world	moment	company
face	love	sea	year	number	government
fact	man	ship	body	paper	president
girl	mark	side	business	person	supply
hand	mile	smile	city	power	

EXERCISE 12 Practice by saying the following sentence, substituting *a* or *the* in the first blank and a noun from Exercise 11 in the second blank. Stress the noun.

That's _____ _____.

EXERCISE 13 Say the words in the list below, first, with *an* in front of them and, then, with *the* in front of them; for instance, *an act – the act.* (Before a following vowel, *the* is usually pronounced [ðɪ].)

act	egg	effort	ocean	enemy	attempt
age	end	honor	office	industry	experience
air	inch	interest	order	officer	idea
arm	action	island	uncle	account	opinion
ear	answer	issue	animal	affair	American
earth	army	object	article	amount	

EXERCISE 14 Practice by saying the following sentence, substituting a noun from Exercise 13 in the blank. Stress the noun.

That's an _____.

LESSON 11 Group Stress: Possessive Adjectives

The possessive adjectives *my, our, your, his, her, its,* and *their* are usually not stressed. Also, the words *his* and *her* are usually pronounced without the *h* unless they come at the beginning of a sentence.

EXERCISE 15 Say the nouns in Exercises 11 and 13 above, putting a possessive adjective before them; for instance, *my book* and *our act.* Be sure to lengthen the stressed vowels in the noun.

EXERCISE 16 Practice by saying the following sentence, substituting a possessive adjective in the first blank and a noun from Exercises 11 and 13 in the second blank. Stress the noun.

That's _____ _____.

LESSON 12 Voiced and Voiceless

Your vocal cords are in your Adam's apple. Your Adam's apple is the hard, angular piece of bone that sticks out on your neck. You can feel it with your fingers. It moves up and down when you swallow.

Make the sound [m]. Close your lips, and let your breath come out through your nose slowly. Put your fingers on your Adam's apple. You can feel a vibration. That vibration makes a sound *voiced.*

Close your lips, and let your breath come out strongly through your nose. Feel your Adam's apple. There should be no vibration there. A sound that is made without noticeable vibration of the vocal cords is a *voiceless* sound.

All the vowels are voiced. They are made with vibration of the vocal cords. Make the sound [ɑ], like the first vowel in the word *father.* Open your mouth wide. Feel your Adam's apple. Make the sound [i], like the first sound in the word *eat.* Open your mouth only a little. Feel your Adam's apple. Both [ɑ] and [i] are voiced.

The voiceless consonants are made with more volume of breath than the voiced consonants: the voiceless consonants are "aspirated." You can think of the voiceless consonants as "strong" sounds and the voiced consonants as "soft" sounds.

There are eight pairs of consonants in English that are different only by the presence or lack of vibration. Whenever you pronounce the following sounds, make the voiced consonants soft, and the voiceless consonants strong.

Voiced		*Voiceless*	
[v]	– vase	[f]	– face
[ð]	– either	[θ]	– ether
[z]	– zeal	[s]	– seal
[ʒ]	– allusion	[ʃ]	– Aleutian
[dʒ]	– gin	[tʃ]	– chin
[b]	– buy	[p]	– pie
[d]	– dime	[t]	– time
[g]	– gold	[k]	– cold

EXERCISE 17 Practice the following, applying the principles previously discussed.

1. She put her face close to the vase.
2. You can have either chloroform or ether.
3. Trappers hunt seals with zeal.
4. The lecturer made an allusion to the Aleutian Islands.
5. You've spilled some gin on your chin.
6. I'm going to buy a pie.
7. I don't have time to spend a dime.
8. Gold usually feels cold.

REVIEW: DIALOGS 16-20

16. 1 – Pardon me.
     Do you have a match?
    2 – Yes, I do.
     Here, help yourself.
    1 – Thank you very much.
    2 – Not at all.

17. 1 — What time is the plane supposed to arrive?
    2 — Six-thirty, but it's behind schedule.
       Now they're saying six-fifty.
    1 — Then we've still got fifteen minutes.

18. 1 — I'd like to look at your shirts.
    2 — Any particular style?
    1 — Could I see what you have?
    2 — Certainly, sir.
       What color did you have in mind?
    1 — White, I think.

19. 1 — Could we have a table for two?
    2 — Yes, sir.
       There's a nice table right over there.
    1 — Thank you.
       May we have the menu?
    2 — Right away, sir.

20. 1 — When should we start the work?
    2 — Let's do it tomorrow.
    1 — What time do you have in mind?
    2 — How about ten o'clock?
    1 — That's fine.
       See you tomorrow.

REVIEW: QUOTATIONS 14-17

14. Alas for the rarity
    Of Christian charity.

    — *Hood*

15. I slept and dreamed that life was beauty;
    I woke and found that life was duty.

    — *Hooper*

16. Life is a jest, and all things show it;
    I thought so once, but now I know it.

    — *Gay*

17. The world is a comedy to those that think,
    a tragedy to those who feel.

    — *Walpole*

Six consonants are made by action of the lips. The lips are closed for [m], [b], and [p]. The lower lip touches the edges of the upper front teeth for [v] and [f]. The lips are rounded for [w].

If you have difficulty with [w], you should practice making it by rounding and slightly extending your lips. Keep your lips away from your teeth. Make sure that you do not suddenly pull your lower lip under the upper teeth. You can also practice by first pronouncing [u] and then adding another vowel – for example, [u...i], [u...e], and [u...o]. Now say them together, and stress the second vowel: [wi], [we], [wo].

[w] occurs only before vowels. For [w], round your lips.

When you pronounce [b], be sure to close your lips firmly.

When you pronounce [v], do not close your lips. Do not round your lips.

EXERCISE 18 Practice the following, applying the principles previously discussed.

mail – bale – pale – wail – veil – fail
main – bane – pain – wane – vain – feign
mare – bear – pair – wear – vair – fair
mile – bile – pile – wile – vile – file
mine – bine – pine – wine – vine – fine
mere – beer – peer – we're – veer – fear
mend – bend – penned – wend – vend – fend
merry – berry – Perry – wary – very – ferry
mind – bind – pined – wind – vined – find
my – buy – pie – Y – vie – fie
mace – base – pace – Wace – vase – face

EXERCISE 19 Practice the following, applying the principles previously discussed.

1. My mother buys pies.
2. Perry is very merry.
3. I got a bale of mail this morning.
4. I can't bear to wear wool next to my skin.
5. That's a fine wine.
6. The wind wailed in the pine trees.
7. Do women wear veils very often?
8. He took a vow never to drink wine or beer.

LESSON 14   Difference in Stress

The following pairs of words are spelled the same, but the stress on the nouns differs from that on the verbs (the adjectives *perfect* and *present* are stressed like the nouns).   The nouns are stressed on the first syllable; lengthen the first syllable.   The verbs are stressed on the second syllable; lengthen the second syllable.

NOUN	VERB	NOUN	VERB
annex	annex	convoy	convoy
concert	concert	decrease	decrease
conduct	conduct	desert	desert
conflict	conflict	digest	digest
contest	contest	exploit	exploit
contract	contract	incline	incline
contrast	contrast	perfect	perfect
convert	convert	present	present

EXERCISE 20   Practice the following, applying the principles previously discussed.

1. The library's in the annex.
2. He'll conduct you to your room.
3. You mustn't break a contract.
4. He contrasted his present home with his former one.
5. The ships went in a convoy.
6. Do you know where the Sahara Desert is?
7. I'm inclined to agree with you.
8. She made a perfect score.
9. Did you hear the concert last night?
10. He contested her statement.
11. She found a conflict in her schedule.
12. You'll have to convert your money into dollars.
13. The merchant decreased his prices.
14. Some people like *The Reader's Digest*.
15. Farmers exploit the land.
16. The group presented him with a gift.

23

EXERCISE 21 Review [i] and [ɪ] and [e]. Pronounce the following words, remembering that [i] is tense, [ɪ] is lax, and [e] is tense.

bean – been – bane
deal – dill – dale
feast – fist – faced
feet – fit – fate
keen – kin – cane
leak – lick – lake

meal – mill – mail
peat – pit – pate
read – rid – raid
seek – sick – sake
sheep – ship – shape
steal – still – stale

EXERCISE 22 Practice the following, applying the principles previously discussed.

1. Her shoes don't fit her feet.
2. The ship has a leak.
3. She faced the group and shook her fist.
4. Fate interferes with my life a great deal.
5. He ate dill pickles and beans.
6. Stale food can make you sick.
7. Is he still working at the mill?
8. Did you read your mail this morning?

LESSON 15 Group Stress: *Some and Any*

The words *some* and *any* before nouns are customarily not stressed. Then, they merely suggest indefiniteness. They are quite similar to the articles *a, an,* and *the* since they are usually not emphasized.

However, *some* and *any* are sometimes stressed. Then, they convey special meanings. Stressed *some* suggests contrast; it often means "special" or "certain in contrast with another or others." Stressed *any* suggests emphasis; sometimes it suggests irritation or sarcasm.

It is very important to stress or not stress *some* or *any* correctly. Your listener may misunderstand your intention.

EXERCISE 23 Pronounce the following sentences twice. The first time, do not stress the *some* or *any*. The second time, stress the *some* or *any*. Each sentence will have two different meanings.

1. I have some friends.
2. That man does not have any money.
3. Some girls like that kind of boy.
4. Have you done any work this week?
5. That author has written some good books.
6. Mrs. Adam's guest did not want any more coffee.

24

21. 1 – Could you help me, please?
    2 – Certainly.
        What would you like?
    1 – Could you look at my radiator?
        I think it's leaking.
        At any rate, something's wrong.

22. 1 – It's raining hard right now.
    2 – And we're both carrying packages.
    1 – Why don't we get a taxi?
    2 – I think that's a good idea.
        I hate to carry packages in the rain.

23. 1 – Should we visit Mr. Brown?
    2 – Why not?
        Where's his house?
    1 – It's on Cherry Street.
        It's near the park.
    2 – Should we walk or take a taxi?
    1 – We might as well walk.

24. 1 – Can John play the piano?
    2 – Yes, he can.
        He can sing, too.
    1 – I can't sing at all.
    2 – Neither can I.

25. 1 – Could you lend me a dollar until tomorrow?
    2 – Of course.
        Do you have change for a five?
    1 – I wish I did.
    2 – Well, we can get it changed easily.

REVIEW: QUOTATIONS 18-21

18. I think that I shall never see
    A poem lovely as a tree.

                   – *Kilmer*

19. Once more: speak clearly if you speak at all;
    Carve each word before you let it fall.

                   – *Holmes*

20. The earth keeps some vibration going
There in your heart, and that is you.

—*Masters*

21. Of all the tyrannies of human kind
The worst is that which persecutes the mind.

— *Dryden*

LESSON 16   The Tooth Ridge

In the pronouncing of English sounds, the tooth ridge is very important. The tooth ridge is the projection above and behind the upper front teeth. Put your tongue on the back of your upper front teeth, and then move it upward. Right above the teeth, you will feel the tooth ridge. Continue to move your tongue upward. It will suddenly go straight up: it has left the tooth ridge.

The tooth ridge is important because a number of English sounds are made by the tip of the tongue touching the tooth ridge. Those sounds are [l], [n], [d], and [t].

The sound [l] is made with the tip of the tongue touching the tooth ridge. Your breath comes over the sides of your tongue and out through your lips. You can continue the sound [l]. Take a deep breath of air, put the tip of your tongue against your tooth ridge, and then let all the breath out of your lungs slowly. Don't move the tip of the tongue. Your vocal cords vibrate: [l] is a voiced sound.

The sound [n] is made with the tip of the tongue touching the tooth ridge. Your breath comes out through your nose. Keep your lips open. The sides of your tongue press against the sides of your upper teeth. You can continue the sound [n]. Don't move your tongue until all your breath has come out through your nose. Your vocal cords vibrate: [n] is a voiced sound.

Both [d] and [t] are made by stopping the breath. You put the tip of your tongue on the tooth ridge and the sides of your tongue against the sides of your upper teeth just as you did for [n], but don't let the breath come out through your nose. The difference between [d] and [t] is that [d] is voiced and [t] is voiceless. Your vocal cords vibrate when you make [d], and they do not vibrate when you make [t].

Practice making the sound [o] followed by [l], then by [n], then by [d], and then by [t]. Next, practice making the sounds [lo], [no], [do], and [to].

Be sure to put the tip of your tongue on your tooth ridge, not on the back of your upper front teeth.

Another sound of English is made with the tip of the tongue *near* the tooth ridge. That sound is [r]. Put your tongue into the position of [n], and then bend the tip of your tongue backward just a little. Let your breath come out through your lips. Hold your tongue in that position: the tip close to the tooth ridge, and the sides against the upper side teeth. Don't shake the tip. Don't make a shaking sound in the back of your mouth. Practice making the sound [o] followed by [n] and then followed by [r]. Then say [no] and [ro].

If you have trouble producing a distinction between [l] and [r], do this: move the tip of your tongue *down* quickly when you finish making [l], and move the tip *upward* quickly when you finish making [r].

EXERCISE 24 Practice the following, applying the principles previously discussed.

[l]	[n]	[d]	[t]	[r]
lap	nap	–	tap	rap
law	gnaw	daw	taw	raw
lay	neigh	day	–	ray
lays	neighs	daze	–	raise
leap	–	deep	–	reap
led	Ned	dead	Ted	red
lent	–	dent	tent	rent
lest	nest	–	test	rest
lewd	nude	dude	–	rude
lice	nice	dice	–	ride
limb	–	dim	Tim	rim
lime	–	dime	time	rhyme
line	nine	dine	tine	Rhine
lip	nip	dip	tip	rip

27

EXERCISE 25 Practice the following, applying the principles previously discussed.

1. He took a nap in the afternoon.
2. Do you like raw vegetables?
3. Horses neigh.
4. Raise your hand if you wish to speak.
5. Ned led Ted to the tent.
6. Your car's got a dent in the front fender.
7. That nude statue isn't lewd.
8. A lot of rice is grown in China.
9. He looked over the rim of his glasses.
10. The light's dim in here.
11. He likes to dine at nine.
12. Leave a tip on the table.
13. A taw is a kind of marble.
14. Turn the other tap for cold water.
15. Rap on the table when you pronounce.
16. That's the law.
17. She was in a daze after the accident.
18. When's the next leap year?
19. They're going to raise my rent.
20. Daws like to rest in their nests.
21. You mustn't be rude to people.
22. Do you know how to play dice?
23. Lice aren't nice.
24. The child broke a limb of the tree.
25. Take your time; don't rush.
26. He took a dip in the Rhine.
27. Put your lips together for [b].
28. Tim lay in his mother's lap.

LESSON 17 Two-Syllable Words: Stress on Second Syllable

The following words have stress on the second syllable. When you pronounce them, be sure to lengthen the stressed vowel.

1. [i]   agree, asleep, belief, believe, beneath, between
2. [ɪ]   admit, appear, begin
3. [e]   afraid, arrange, ashamed, awake, away
4. [ɛ]   accept, affair, again, against, ahead, arrest, attempt, collect, compare, confess, connect, correct, declare, defend

5. [æ] advance, attack
6. [ə] above, among
7. [ɑ] adopt, apart
8. [ɔ] abroad, accord, across
9. [o] ago, alone, although
10. [ʊ] insure
11. [u] accuse, amuse, approve
12. [ɚ] concern, confirm
13. [aɪ] admire, advice, advise, alike, alive, apply, arise, arrive
14. [aʊ] about, account
15. [ɔɪ] annoy, appoint

EXERCISE 26 Practice the following, applying the principles previously discussed.

1. He'll agree to anything.
2. She was ashamed of her part in the affair.
3. I'll confess that my belief wasn't correct.
4. They'll arrest the man you accuse.
5. Are we in accord now?
6. She's afraid to go alone.
7. She was asleep beneath the tree.
8. Did the account in the paper amuse you?
9. Do you approve of everything you admire?
10. If we advance, they'll attack.
11. I'll arrange to insure the car.
12. Be prepared to defend anything you say.

LESSON 18 Nasal Sounds

The three sounds [m], [n], and [ŋ] are "nasals" — your breath comes out of your nose when you make them.

You already know how to make the sound [n]: you put the tip of your tongue against your tooth ridge and let your breath come out through your nose. Don't close your lips.

To make [m], you close your lips and let your breath come out through your nose.

To make [ŋ], press the tip of your tongue against your lower front teeth. Keep your lips open. Let your breath come out through your nose. The back of your tongue will go up against the roof of your mouth to prevent your breath from coming out through your mouth.

When you finish making a nasal, don't "explode": don't let your breath come out of your mouth with an audible noise. If you explode after [m], you will probably say [p]; after [n], you will probably say [t]; after [ŋ], you will probably say [k]. Don't explode.

EXERCISE 27 Pronounce the following triplets. Don't explode after the nasal. The final letters *ng* represent [ŋ], don't make a [g] or [k] after the [ŋ].

[m]	[n]	[ŋ]
bam	ban	bang
clam	clan	clang
dim	din	ding
ram	ran	rang
rum	run	rung
some	sun	sung
tam	tan	tang

EXERCISE 28 Practice the following, applying the principles previously discussed

1. There used to be a ban on liquor.
2. Do you like clam chowder?
3. That's the name of an old Scottish clan.
4. The captain tried to ram the other ship.
5. Has the bell rung?
6. The balloon burst with a bang.
7. Nightclubs are usually dim.
8. She's wearing a plaid tam.
9. I can't stand that din.
10. Puerto Rico sells a lot of rum.
11. Do you like to sit in the sun and get a tan?

EXERCISE 29 Review [ɪ] and [e] and [ɛ]. Pronounce the following words, remembering that [ɪ] is lax, [e] is tense, and [ɛ] is lax.

bill – bail – bell	lit – late – let
bit – bait – bet	mitt – mate – met
dill – dale – dell	pin – pain – pen
fill – fail – fell	pit – pate – pet
hill – hail – hell	rick – rake – wreck
ill – ale – *l* (the letter)	rid – raid – red
kin – cane – ken	sill – sail – sell
lid – laid – led	till – tail – tell
list – laced – lest	will – wail – well

EXERCISE 30 Practice the following, applying the principles previously discussed.

1. Pay your bill to the cashier.
2. Write it down lest you forget.
3. A dog bit me once.
4. Don't be late for class.
5. The farmer's in the dell.
6. That baby's going to wail again.
7. I've got something to tell you.
8. I can't get rid of this cold.
9. He caught the ball in his mitt.
10. I hope I didn't fail that exam.
11. Don't put that pot on the window sill.
12. Have you ever seen it hail?
13. People talk about the pit of hell.
14. The food made her ill.
15. I've got to rake the leaves off the lawn.
16. Do you have a straight pin?
17. The enemy made another raid last night.
18. Wait till I tell you to start.
19. Are you kin to that girl?
20. His bald pate shone under the light.

31

26. 1 — Don't you want to study any more?
    2 — Well, I'm getting pretty tired.
       I've had a very long day.
    1 — Then we'd better stop right here.
    2 — We can start on the next page tomorrow.

27. 1 — Why isn't John here yet?
    2 — He's trying to find a place to park.
    1 — It's hard to find places around here.
    2 — It certainly is.
       I know from experience.

28. 1 — I'd like to have this suit cleaned.
       When can I pick it up?
    2 — How soon do you need it, sir?
    1 — I was planning on wearing it Friday.
    2 — No trouble at all, sir.
       It'll be ready on Friday morning.

29. 1 — What's that man's name?
       The man over there with the book.
    2 — It's slipped my memory.
       I know it, but I can't think of it.
       It'll come back to me in a minute.
    1 — Doesn't his name start with an f?
    2 — Yes, I think it does.

30. 1 — Will you be at home next Tuesday?
    2 — I plan to, but I may have to leave town.
    1 — I'd like to talk to you then.
       Can I call you on Tuesday night?
    2 — Surely.

REVIEW: QUOTATIONS 22-25

22. I loaf and invite my soul.
    I lean and loaf at my ease, observing
        a spear of summer grass.
                                    — *Whitman*

23. Life is real! Life is earnest!
    And the grave is not its goal.
                                    — *Longfellow*

24. He that fights and runs away.
May live to fight another day.
— *Anonymous*

25. I must go down to the seas again,
to the lonely sea and the sky,
And all I ask is a tall ship and a
star to steer her by.
— *Masefield*

LESSON 19 Contrastive Stress

Stress is sometimes used to indicate a contrast. For that use, words which are customarily not stressed are stressed, and words which customarily have some stress are given abnormal stress. Sometimes the two parts of the contrast are stated; very often, however, the other part of the contrast is implied.

Since contrastive stress has a meaning, be careful about using it. For example, do not stress pronouns, auxiliaries, and other customarily unstressed words unless you intend to convey an idea of contrast.

EXERCISE 31 Pronounce the following sentences, using contrastive stress on the underlined words.

1. He isn't going, but I am.
2. Put the book on the table, not in the table.
3. In spite of everything, I will go.
4. Paul wants his book, not yours.
5. Mary did not tell me that secret.

LESSON 20 Stop Sounds

The sounds [b], [p], [d], [t], [g], and [k] are made by stopping the breath. For that reason, those sounds are called "stops." [b] and [p] are made by closing the lips. [d] and [t] are made by putting the tip of the tongue against the tooth ridge. [g] and [k] are made by putting the back of the tongue against the velum. [b], [d], and [g] are voiced; [p], [t], and [k] are voiceless.

If one of the stops is the first sound in a word, the breath is suddenly released through the mouth; there is an "explosion." If a stop is between two vowels within a word, the breath is suddenly stopped

33

and then released. If a stop is the last sound in a word, the breath is stopped and is usually *not* released: there is no explosion.

Close your lips and keep them closed to prevent yourself from exploding a final [b] or [p]. Put the tip of your tongue on the tooth ridge and leave it there for a final [d] or [t] (and don't close your lips). Press the back of your tongue against your velum and keep it there for a final [g] or [k] (and don't close your lips).

A final nasal sound also is not exploded; that is, the breath is not released through the mouth. It is very important to remember that with words ending in the letters -*ng*. The spelling -*ng* represents only one sound, [ŋ]. Be sure not to explode at the end of words like *thing* and *reading*.

Voiceless stops are "stronger" than voiced stops: say [p], [t], and [k] with much force; say [b], [d], and [g] gently.

EXERCISE 32 Practice these combinations. Don't explode the stop at the end of the first word.

1. keep back
2. eat carrots
3. about taxes
4. told me
5. rapid delivery
6. like to
7. sat down
8. that girl
9. lagging behind
10. going to
11. black pencil
12. bought none

EXERCISE 33 Practice these pairs. Lengthen the vowel before [b]. Shorten the vowel before [p] Don't explode a final stop.

path – bath	rapid – rabid	rip – rib
peer – beer	staple – stable	gap – gab
peas – bees		lap – lab
palm – bomb		tap – tab

EXERCISE 34 Practice the following, applying the principles previously discussed.

1. She's taking a bath.
2. He drinks a lot of beer.
3. I hate peas and carrots.
4. He held the kitten in his palm.

EXERCISE 34 (Continued)

5. Mr. Carter's rabid about taxes.
6. The Bible says Eve was made from Adam's rib.
7. There's a gap in the wall.
8. He's working in the chemistry lab.
9. That tap's leaking.
10. There's a path to the next building.
11. He's a peer in England.
12. He told me about the birds and bees.
13. They keep talking about the atom bomb.
14. That store boasts about its rapid delivery.
15. Did you rip your shirt?
16. Those two women like to sit and gab.

EXERCISE 35 Practice these pairs. Lengthen the vowel before [d]. Shorten the vowel before [t]. Don't explode a final stop.

team – deem	bright – bride	fright – fried
tale – dale	built – build	great – grade
teen – dean	cart – card	halt – hauled
time – dime	cat – cad	let – led
tin – din	feet – feed	mate – made
	set – said	

EXERCISE 36 Practice the following, applying the principles previously discussed.

1. He's the captain of the football team.
2. Do you believe that tale?
3. It used to cost a dime to ride the subway.
4. He left his calling card.
5. She called him a cad.
6. He fried an egg.
7. The policeman told him to halt.
8. I deem it's all right.
9. He's in his teens now.
10. The bride was very pretty.
11. When are they going to build that new factory?
12. I've got to feed the animals.
13. What was your grade?
14. Let me see what you've made.

35

EXERCISE 37 Practice these pairs. Lengthen the vowel before [g]. Shorten the vowel before [k]. Don't explode a final stop.

cab – gab	lacking – lagging	buck – bug
cad – gad	meeker – meager	chuck – chug
cap – gap	discussed – disgust	lack – lag
card – guard		leak – league
come – gum		luck – lug
cold – gold		rack – rag
crew – grew		tack – tag

EXERCISE 38 Practice the following, applying the principles previously discussed.

1. Let's go by cab.
2. He took off his cap and sat down.
3. He grew meeker as his wife talked more.
4. Polish it with a rag.
5. I hope you have good luck.
6. She found a bug in her bed.
7. That girl loves to gad about.
8. You're lagging behind the other students.
9. They're going to form a league.
10. She hung the picture on a tack.
11. He says he's going to chuck his job.
12. The crew abandoned the ship.

EXERCISE 39 Practice pronouncing the following words with [g] and [ŋ]. Don't explode a final stop.

bag – bang	rig – ring	sag – sang
log – long		sprig – spring
rag – rang		wig – wing

EXERCISE 40 Practice the following, applying the principles previously discussed.

1. What've you got in that bag?
2. The butler came when she rang.
3. Stand up straight; don't sag
4. She wears a white wig in the play.
5. I won't be gone long.
6. They're drilling for oil with a rig.
7. He broke off a sprig from the bush.
8. They stood under the wing of the plane.

EXERCISE 41 Practice pronouncing the following words with [n] and [ŋ]. Don't explode a final stop.

ban – bang	sinner – singer	ran – rang
been – bing		robin – robbing
clan – clang		run – rung
din – ding		sin – sing
fan – fang		sun – sung
gone – gong		tan – tang
kin – king		thin – thing
lawn – long		ton – tongue
pan – pang		win – wing

EXERCISE 42 Practice the following, applying the principles previously discussed.

1. Where've you been?
2. I saw a robin this morning.
3. Do you like Bing Crosby?
4. Has the bell rung?
5. It's no sin to like that.
6. He felt a pang of regret about going.
7. A snake releases its poison through its fangs.
8. Change classes when you hear the gong.
9. That boy's too thin.
10. I wouldn't like to be a king.
11. Stick out your tongue.
12. The airplane's wing caught fire.
13. Don't try to look at the sun at noon.
14. He ran when I called him.
15. Oranges have a sharp tang.

EXERCISE 43 Practice pronouncing the following words with [m] and [n]. Don't explode a final stop.

map – nap	dim – din	seem – seen
me – knee	rum – run	some – sun
mine – nine	same – sane	them – then
might – night		tome – tone

EXERCISE 44 Practice the following, applying the principles previously discussed.

1. Things are not always what they seem.
2. What happened then?
3. If you need a raincoat, take mine.
4. I didn't like the tone of your voice when you said that.
5. I can't find that country on the map.
6. That was a sane remark.
7. He cut his knee when he fell.
8. It's exactly the same.
9. Why didn't you take some?

LESSON 21   Three-Syllable Words: Stress on First Syllable

The following words have stress on the first syllable. When you pronounce them, be sure to lengthen the stressed vowel.

1. [i]   eagerly, easily
2. [ɪ]   bitterness, citizen, civilize, criminal, critical, difficult, discipline
3. [e]   agency, favorable
4. [ɛ]   anyhow, anything, anyway, anywhere, century, definite, delicate, educate, elephant, enemy, envious, estimate, everything, everywhere
5. [æ]   actively, actual, advertise, accident, animal, avenue, calculate, camera
6. [ə]   company, cultivate, customer, government
7. [ɑ]   argument, article, colony, commonly, confidence, confident, conqueror, consciousness
8. [ɔ]   audience, formerly, fortunate
9. [o]   nobody
10. [ʊ]   curious
11. [u]   beautiful
12. [ɚ]   certainly, circular
13. [aɪ]   bicycle, library
14. [aʊ]   nowadays

EXERCISE 45 Practice the following, applying the principles previously discussed.

1. She waited eagerly for his return.
2. His estimate was higher than the actual cost.
3. An elephant isn't a delicate animal.
4. She lost consciousness when she heard about his accident.
5. The conqueror captured the colony easily.
6. Your argument is circular.
7. Should we try to educate all citizens?
8. A criminal lacks discipline.
9. The audience seemed favorable.
10. He's curious about everything.
11. The company is going to advertise its new camera.
12. He certainly has a lot of confidence in himself.
13. He rode his bicycle down the avenue.
14. An envious person is filled with bitterness.

REVIEW: DIALOGS 31-35

31. 1 — What's that man's name?
    2 — Frederick Adams.
    1 — When was he born?
    2 — In 1930 — August 10, 1930.
    1 — Is he married?
    2 — No, he's still a bachelor.

32. 1 — Do you want me to wait here?
    2 — No, you go ahead.
        I think I can handle everything.
    1 — All right then.
        I'll meet you later.
    2 — Yes, in just a few minutes.

33. 1 — I think you're going to be late.
    2 — I'm going as fast as I can.
        How much time is there left?
    1 — You've got about ten minutes.
    2 — I'll be ready in six or seven.

34. 1 — Are you sure you didn't put it there?
    2 — I don't think so.
    Would you look again?
    1 — I'll take another look, but I don't think it's here.
    2 — I hope it is.

35. 1 — I've got a belief about the weather.
    2 — What is it?
    1 — Winters are getting colder.
    2 — Can you prove it?

REVIEW: QUOTATIONS 26-28

26. Damn with faint praise; assent with civil leer,
    And, without sneering, teach the rest to sneer.

    — Pope

27. I have had playmates; I have had companions,
    In my days of childhood, in my joyful school-days;
    All, all are gone, the old, familiar faces.

    — Lamb

28. O Captain! my Captain! our fearful trip is done,
    The ship has weathered every rack, the prize
    we sought is won,
    The port is near, the bells I hear, the people
    all exulting.

    — Whitman

LESSON 22   Stop Sounds with Gentle Explosion

A final stop [p, t, k, b, d, g] is exploded if it follows another stop or a nasal [m, n, ŋ], as in *stamp, land,* or *think.* The reason is that the breath has been stopped from coming out of the mouth by the preceding sound. If the final stop were not exploded, it would not be heard. However, do not explode such a final stop violently; explode gently. Lengthen vowels before voiced stops; shorten them before voiceless ones.

EXERCISE 46 Practice these pairs. Lengthen the vowels before [nd]; shorten them before [nt]. Explode the [t] and [d] gently.

bent – bend	joint – joined	rent – rend
complaint – complained	lent – lend	restraint – restrained
extent – extend	meant – mend	sent – send
grant – grand	paint – pained	spent – spend
	plant – planned	

EXERCISE 47 Practice the following, applying the principles previously discussed.

1. Bend over, and let me look at your hair.
2. He was bent with age.
3. What's your complaint?
4. He complained, but nothing happened.
5. What was the extent of the damage?
6. Extend your left arm.
7. He got a grant for his tuition.
8. I'm feeling grand.
9. He joined the group a few years ago.
10. Let's make it a joint effort.
11. Banks charge interest on what they lend.
12. He repaid the money I lent him.
13. That's not what I meant.
14. You'd better mend your ways.
15. They're going to paint our apartment.
16. He had a pained expression on his face.
17. It didn't turn out the way we'd planned.
18. Are you going to plant those seeds?
19. Do you have to pay high rent?
20. Actresses sometimes rend their clothes.
21. Children often need to be restrained.
22. He talked without restraint.
23. Did you get the note I sent?
24. What'll we send?
25. Don't spend more than you earn.
26. She's spent all her money.

EXERCISE 48 Practice pronouncing the following words with final [nd] and [ŋd]. Explode gently.

band – banged   hand – hanged   clanned – clanged

EXERCISE 49 Practice the following, applying the principles previously discussed.

1. She held out her hand.
2. The murderer was finally hanged.
3. Have you heard the band?
4. The swinging door banged.
5. The people in that village have clanned together.
6. Both the cymbals were clanged together.

EXERCISE 50 Practice pronouncing the following words with final [ŋ] and [ŋk]. Explode the second word of each pair gently.

bang – bank	ping – pink	sling – slink
bring – brink	rang – rank	sting – stink
bung – bunk	ring – rink	sung – sunk
clang – clank	sang – sank	tang – tank
king – kink	sing – sink	thing – think
Ming – mink		wing – wink

EXERCISE 51 Practice the following, applying the principles previously discussed.

1. The firecracker exploded with a bang.
2. When you go to camp, you may sleep on a bunk.
3. The Ming dynasty lasted until the seventeenth century.
4. What was his rank in the army?
5. Put the dishes in the sink.
6. Did a bee ever sting you?
7. Every tall building has a water tank on the roof.
8. Are we on the brink of war?
9. He heard their chains clank.
10. The rope's got a kink.
11. That's a pretty pink dress.
12. I'll give you a ring tomorrow.
13. The soprano sang beautifully.
14. His arm's in a sling.
15. The ship may have been sunk.
16. Life's just one thing after another.
17. You shouldn't wink at girls.

42

EXERCISE 52 Practice pronouncing the following words with final [ŋɪŋ] and [ŋkɪŋ]. Don't explode the final sound.

banging – banking   singing – sinking   stinging – stinking
clanging – clanking   slinging – slinking   winging – winking

EXERCISE 53 Practice the following, applying the principles previously discussed.

1. I wish that child would stop banging his drum.
2. He was singing at the top of his voice.
3. Her eyes were stinging from the salt water.
4. The clanging of the fire engine woke me up.
5. I saw a wolf slinking near the house.
6. Birds will be winging their way north soon.

EXERCISE 54 Practice these pairs. Lengthen the vowel before [ŋz]; shorten it before [ŋks].

bangs – banks   kings – kinks   stings – stinks
brings – brinks   rings – rinks   things – thinks
clangs – clanks   sings – sinks   wings – winks
                    slings – slinks

EXERCISE 55 Practice the following, applying the principles previously discussed.

1. Her bangs keep getting into her eyes.
2. The town has two skating rinks.
3. That cut on my finger still stings.
4. I've got a number of things to tell you.
5. He brings his wife a surprise every evening.
6. Do angels have wings?
7. She loves to show off her rings.
8. Are the banks closed now?

LESSON 23   -NG with Inflections

-ng is exploded [ŋg] before the comparison inflections -er and -est as in *longer – longest* and *stronger – strongest*. -ng is not exploded before any other inflection, including -er meaning agent — for example, *singer, stringy,* and *bringing.*

EXERCISE 56 Practice the following, applying the principles previously discussed.

1. I have been here longer than you have.
2. My father is the strongest man in the world.
3. The singer sang a beautiful song.
4. The banker is bringing the things now.
5. If your hair gets wet, it will look stringy.

EXERCISE 57 Review [e] and [ɛ] and [æ]. Pronounce the following words, remembering [e] is tense, [ɛ] is lax, and [æ] is tense.

bait – bet – bat	mace – mess – mass
caped – kept – capped	main – men – man
fade – fed – fad	mate – met – mat
flakes – flex – flax	pain – pen – pan
gate – get – gat	paste – pest – past
lace – less – lass	pate – pet – pat
laced – lest – last	rain – wren – ran
laid – led – lad	rake – wreck – rack
later – letter – latter	sate – set – sat

EXERCISE 58 Practice the following, applying the principles previously discussed.

1. He picked up the baseball bat.
2. His room is in a mess.
3. Do you have a pet?
4. When he was a young lad, he was very good-looking.
5. Do you like corn flakes?
6. Don't take the pie out of the pan until it's cool.
7. Please set the table.
8. I'm making less than I used to.
9. Paste the notice on the board.
10. That's just a passing fad.
11. Put a mat under the vase.
12. A wren is a brown bird.
13. See you later.
14. Put your hat on the rack.
15. He opened the gate for the horses.

36. 1 – You look serious.
       What's the matter?
    2 – I don't have any sympathy for students who don't study.
    1 – Is that what's bothering you?
    2 – Yes, it is.
       Does that satisfy your curiosity?

37. 1 – You shaved this morning, didn't you?
    2 – Why, yes, I did.
       I usually do.
    1 – You must have cut your chin.
    2 – Yes, I did.
       The razor was very sharp.

38. 1 – Let's go swimming in the pool.
    2 – I wish I could, but I can't.
       I've got to study for an examination.
    1 – It's a shame you can't.
    2 – Maybe we can go tomorrow.

39. 1 – Did your visitor get off all right?
    2 – Yes, he did.
       We didn't have any time to spare, though.
    1 – But he made it?
    2 – Yes, he caught the train just as it was leaving.

40. 1 – I've got to go downtown.
    2 – What for?
    1 – To meet a friend.
       How do I get there from here?
    2 – Take the subway.
       It's by far the fastest way.

REVIEW: QUOTATIONS 29-30

29. And the night shall be filled with music,
    And the cares that infest the day
    Shall fold their tents, like the Arabs,
    And as silently steal away.

    – Longfellow

30. "You are old, Father William," the young man said,
       "And your hair has become very white,
    And yet you incessantly stand on your head.
       Do you think, at your age, it is right?"

    – Carroll

45

LESSON 24 The Past Form

The pronunciation of the past tense or past participle of most verbs follows a very regular system. One of three sounds is added to present tense or simple form of a "regular" verb according to the last *sound* of that form:

1. If the last sound of the simple form is [t] or [d], add the sound [ɪd].

2. If the last sound of the simple form is a voiceless sound other than [t], add the sound [t]. The voiceless sounds in which such a simple form may end are [p], [k], [f], [θ], [s], [ʃ], and [tʃ].

3. If the last sound of the simple form is a voiced sound other than [d], add the sound [d]. The voiced sounds in which such a simple form may end are the vowels, diphthongs, and [b], [g], [m], [n], [ŋ], [v], [ð], [l], [r], [z], [ʒ], and [dʒ].

EXERCISE 59 Add the sound [ɪd] to the following simple forms:

accept	crowd	imitate	nod	report
add	descend	include	paint	succeed
amend	divide	interest	persuade	surround
assist	elect	invite	protect	suspect
attend	excite	land	provide	taste
concede	extend	offend	remind	test
connect	fade	operate	rent	yield

EXERCISE 60 Add the sound [t] to the following simple forms:

address	cough	increase	mix	replace
ask	develop	kiss	pack	touch
clap	drop	kick	pick	wish
cook	erase	laugh	reach	work

EXERCISE 61 Add the sound [d] to the following simple forms:

accustom	circle	explain	oppose	remain
agree	consider	fill	pay	rule
beg	continue	judge	play	satisfy
believe	desire	learn	postpone	supply
charge	discover	observe	refuse	suppose

46

EXERCISE 62 Practice the following, applying the principles previously discussed.

1. I've persuaded Sarah to go.
2. You haven't connected the radio.
3. He accepted the present.
4. I've asked you a question.
5. The mother kissed her child.
6. The speaker addressed the gathering.
7. Watt invented the steam engine.
8. I agreed to his proposal.
9. Mr. Jones continued his journey.
10. She begged him to stop.
11. I'm interested in English.
12. The waiter added up the bill.
13. Was Jim included in the party?
14. You've picked the wrong answer.
15. She's already tasted the candy.
16. I'm supposed to leave tomorrow.
17. He's learned his lesson.
18. I've worked here for years.
19. She circled the mistake with a red pencil.
20. The boy remained silent.
21. She filled the pitcher with water.
22. The club elected him president.
23. Their house hasn't been painted for years.
24. He packed his bags.
25. The store replaced the broken dish.
26. The policeman reported the accident.
27. He's considered to be a fair teacher.
28. Are you excited about going?
29. Mr. Whitson judged the case.
30. The teacher explained the problem.
31. She paid her fare.
32. We rented a new apartment.
33. Have you got accustomed to living here?
34. The men crowded into the room.
35. Have you tested the water?
36. His boss increased his salary.
37. Have you discovered your error?
38. That record is being played everywhere.

39. She desired nothing more.
40. He refused my offer.
41. They believed everything I told them.
42. The referee ruled the game a tie.
43. Are you satisfied with your grade?
44. She charged the dress to her husband.
45. He dropped the vase.
46. Have you been supplied with all your needs?

LESSON 25 Three-Syllable Words: Stress on Second Syllable

The following words have stress on the second syllable. When you pronounce them, be sure to lengthen the stressed vowel.

1. [i] agreement, convenience
2. [ɪ] admission, ambition, ambitious, appearance, artistic, beginning, committee, condition, consider, continue
3. [e] arrangement, behavior
4. [ɛ] adventure, already, attention, attentive, collection, confession, connection, contented, correction, dependent, descendant, develop, direction, directly, director
5. [æ] advantage, attraction, attractive, companion
6. [ə] accustom, another, destruction, destructive
7. [a] adopted, adoption
8. [ɔ] according
9. [o] explosion, explosive
10. [ʊ] insurance
11. [u] amusement, approval
12. [ɚ] commercial, concerning
13. [aɪ] arrival, delightful, entirely
14. [aʊ] allowance
15. [ɔɪ] annoyance, appointment, avoidance

EXERCISE 63 Practice the following, applying the principles previously discussed.

1. That's not according to our agreement.
2. The insurance company paid for it.
3. Don't be late for your appointment.
4. A committee will consider your application for admission.

5. You should be attentive in class.
6. The Browns have adopted a baby boy.
7. Do you feel ambitious?
9. You'll have to get his approval.
9. The explosion caused a lot of damage.
10. He kept his attention on the director.
11. She has an attractive appearance.
12. Let's continue the arrangement.
13. I've a confession to make.
14. His annoyance was beginning to show.
15. His descendants still live in the house.

LESSON 26   The -day Words

The names of the days of the week and the word *yesterday* are all stressed on the first syllable, and they all end in unstressed [dɪ] in ordinary conversation. The word *today* is stressed on the second syllable, and the first syllable is pronounced [tə]. Be sure to put your tongue on your tooth ridge for the [t] and [d] in those words. Practice: *Monday, Tuesday, Wednesday, Thursday, Friday, Saturday, Sunday, yesterday, today.*

EXERCISE 64   Review group stress. Stress the noun: lengthen the stressed vowel. Don't stop between the words of the group.

to a movie	the weather	your homework
over the world	a book	in the library
of ways	in Washington	my wife
a belief	of the week	the way
about the weather	of our worries	by our bodies
the subway	the wind	with the bells
to bed	the bells	our lives
without the words	of cabbages	an achievement
by the weight	on his back	with a beard
in the breeze	in the world	in a way

LESSON 27   Intervocalic t

Sometimes a *t* sounds like a *d*. That happens in ordinary speaking when the *t* comes between two voiced sounds. For example, *matter* may sound like *madder*, *atom* like *Adam*, *twenty* like *twendy*, *little* like

LESSON 27 (Continued)

liddle, city like *ciddy,* and *butter* like *budder.* When people speak slowly or emphatically, however, they usually pronounce that kind of a *t* like [t] and not like [d]. Also, a *t* does not sound like [d] when it precedes a stressed vowel, as in *return,* or when it comes after a voiceless consonant, as in *after.*

EXERCISE 65 Review [ɛ] and [æ] and [ə]. Pronounce the following words, remembering that [ɛ] is lax, [æ] is tense, [ə] is lax.

beg – bag – bug	met – mat – mutt
bet – bat – but	peck – pack – puck
dead – dad – dud	pen – pan – pun
leg – lag – lug	pep – pap – pup
guess – gas – Gus	ten – tan – ton
lest – last – lust	wren – ran – run
mess – mass – muss	guest – gassed – gust
messed – mast – must	

EXERCISE 65 Practice the following, applying the principles previously discussed.

1. I beg your pardon.
2. That bomb wasn't a dud.
3. This is your last chance.
4. Please don't muss my hair.
5. Where's my pack of cigarets?
6. I haven't got much pep today.
7. How does that song run?
8. Which team did you bet on?
9. There's been a lag in production recently.
10. My dog's only a mutt, but I love him.
11. Do you know a pun in your language?
12. He ordered a ton of coal.

REVIEW: DIALOGS 41-45

41. 1 – I have to go to Florida next week.
    2 – Why do you have to go?
    1 – For business reasons.
    2 – How will you make the trip – by train or by plane?
    1 – I'll probably go by plane.

42. 1— You certainly look healthy.
    Have you put on weight?
    2— Yes, I think I have.
    I don't get enough exercise.
    1— Neither do I, but I watch my diet.

43. 1— I'd like to invite you and your wife to dinner.
    Could you come tonight?
    2— Yes, that would be very nice.
    At your house?
    1— Yes. At seven o'clock.

44. 1— Do you have any plans for tomorrow?
    2— Nothing definite.
    1— How would you like to go on a picnic?
    2— That sounds like a lot of fun.
    1— We'd be glad to have you come.
    2— I'll be glad to.

45. 1— What do you want to do now?
    2— Would you like to see a movie?
    1— I don't think so.
    I saw one last night.
    2— Let's go to the library then.

REVIEW: QUOTATIONS 31-32

31. Fame is what you have taken;
    Character is what you give;
    When to this truth you waken,
    Then you begin to live.

    — *Taylor*

32. I never saw a purple cow;
    I never hope to see one;
    But I can tell you anyhow
    I'd rather see than be one.

    — *Burgess*

Four sounds are made by putting the tip of the tongue near the front teeth: [s], [z], [ʃ], and [ʒ]. Don't touch the teeth, however.

To make a distinction between the sounds, try this: put the tip of your tongue close to the upper front teeth for [s] and [z], and put the tip close to the lower front teeth for [ʃ] and [ʒ]. You can also protrude your lips for [ʃ] and [ʒ].

You touch the tooth ridge when you make [tʃ] and [dʒ]. Touch the ridge with your tongue-tip and quickly move the tip downward.

The sounds [s], [ʃ], and [tʃ] are voiceless. The sounds [z], [ʒ], and [dʒ] are voiced. As an aid to your production of these sounds, think of the voiceless ones as "strong" and the voiced ones as "soft." Push your breath out strongly when you say [s], [ʃ], and [tʃ]; let it out gently when you say [z], [ʒ], and [dʒ].

EXERCISE 67 Practice pronouncing the following words with [s] and [ʃ] and [tʃ]. For [s], put the tip of your tongue close to your upper teeth; for [ʃ], put it close to your lower teeth. Don't stop your breath for either of those sounds. For [tʃ], stop your breath by putting the tip of your tongue on your tooth ridge, and then quickly release it by moving the tip down towards your lower teeth. [s], [ʃ], and [tʃ] are all voiceless; make them "strong."

seat – sheet – cheat	sews – shows – chose
seer – sheer – cheer	Swiss – swish – switch
sip – ship – chip	seep – sheep – cheap
sop – shop – chop	sin – shin – chin
mass – mash – match	sues – shoes – choose
sock – shock – chock	lass – lash – latch
sees – she's – cheese	lease – leash – leech
sue – shoe – chew	

EXERCISE 68 Practice the following, applying the principles previously discussed.

1. Please sit in that seat.
2. You'd better shut the windows and latch them.

3. Please switch off the light when you leave.
4. A prophet is a seer.
5. Mr. Chin isn't related to Mr. Shin.
6. Chew your food thoroughly before you swallow it.
7. She sews very well.
8. You'll get a shock from that socket.
9. Are you going to the boxing match tonight?
10. That's cheap at any price.
11. She's eaten all the cheese.
12. Do you like chipped beef?
13. Those aren't the shoes I'd choose.
14. He's got to chop some wood for the fire.
15. I'm not going to renew the lease on my apartment.

EXERCISE 69 Practice pronouncing the following words with [s] and [z]. Put your tongue tip close to your upper teeth for both sounds. Make [s] a "strong" sound; make [z] a "soft" sound.

seal – zeal	fussy – fuzzy	cease – seize
see – z	lacy – lazy	ice – eyes
sing – zing		loose – lose
sink – zinc		once – ones
sip – zip		peace – peas
sown – zone		price – prize
sue – zoo		rice – rise
seize – z's		

EXERCISE 70 Practice the following, applying the principles previously discussed.

1. He always does his work with zeal.
2. He likes to sing.
3. She took a sip of coffee.
4. Her name's Susan, but we call her Sue.
5. She used the lacy tablecloth for dinner.
6. She opened her eyes and yawned.
7. Did you lose something?
8. She bought a can of peas.
9. What's the price of eggs today?
10. Z is the last letter of the American-English alphabet.

11. Does zinc sink?
12. Don't stop in a no-parking zone.
13. Don't be so fussy about unimportant details.
14. The government's going to seize the coal mines.
15. You take the big ones, and I'll take the little ones.
16. Let's have rice with the chicken.

LESSON 29 The -S Inflection

The inflection or suffix -s has three different uses:

1. To show the third-person singular, present tense of most verbs.
2. To show the plural of most nouns.
3. To show possession of many nouns.

The spelling for the first two uses is similar. For most words we add an s. We add es when a word ends in the letters s, z, sh, or x. We add es after the letters ch pronounced [tʃ], but s after ch pronounced [k]. We add es when a final y is changed to i.

The spelling for the possessive can be simplified to this:

1. Add 's if the word does not end in the letter s.
2. Add only the apostrophe if the word ends in s.

The pronunciation of the inflection (-s, -'s, or es) follows a regular system:

1. The inflection is pronounced [ɪz] if the preceding sound is [s], [z], [ʃ], [ʒ], [tʃ], or [dʒ]. Such a sound is called a **sibilant**.

2. The inflection is pronounced [s] if the preceding sound is [p], [t], [k], [f], or [θ]. Such a sound is a **voiceless non-sibilant**.

3. The inflection is pronounced [z] is the preceding sound is not one of those listed above. That sound may be a vowel, a diphthong, or [b], [d], [g], [v], [ð], [l], [r], [m], [n], or [ŋ]. Such a sound is a **voiced non-sibilant**.

EXERCISE 71 Add the sound [ɪz] to the following words:

accuse	cause	manage	possess	sacrifice
address	change	match	promise	stretch
advance	dress	memorize	pronounce	supervise
advise	encourage	mix	propose	surprise
announce	establish	notice	publish	switch
arrange	judge	oppose	recognize	watch

EXERCISE 72 Add the sound [s] to the following words. Make the [s] with much force. The combination -sts, as in *exists*, is customarily pronounced as a prolonged [s].

accept	correct	knock	provoke	stamp
ache	develop	last	request	stop
act	drop	omit	resent	want
attack	exist	point	revoke	waste
check	expect	predict	risk	wipe
complete	faint	print	shout	wrap

EXERCISE 73 Add the sound [z] to the following words. Make the [z] with little force.

admire	bury	curve	enter	move
aim	cheer	dare	evade	need
appear	clean	defend	extend	observe
approve	command	describe	fail	recommend
assign	compare	deserve	guard	renew
assume	conceal	destroy	happen	reveal
avoid	control	die	imagine	study
believe	cry	enjoy	inquire	supply

LESSON 30   The 's Contraction

The contraction 's for the words *is* and *has* is pronounced like the inflection s. After a word ending with a voiceless non-sibilant, 's is pronounced [s].

1. The shop's empty.   2. It's been shut for a week.

After a word ending with a voiced non-sibilant, 's is pronounced [z]:

1. The man's in New York.   2. He's been there since Monday.

After a word ending with a sibilant, the contraction is not used. *Is* is pronounced [ɪz]. Stressed *has* is pronounced [hæz], and unstressed *has* is pronounced [əz]:

1. English is easy.   2. My wish has come true.

EXERCISE 74 Practice the following, applying the principles previously discussed.

1. Today's the first day of school.
2. It's very warm today.
3. The weather's nice today.
4. Do you think English is easy?
5. What's the matter?
6. That's a nice-looking hat.
7. When's the next test?
8. Where's the post office?
9. There's something that's bothering me.
10. She's the spirit of the school.
11. A pretty girl's like a melody.
12. The best one's the one you like most.
13. He's got to go down town.
14. George has lost his job.
15. No news is good news.
16. All's well that ends well.
17. Your hair's become very white.
18. The time's come.

EXERCISE 75 Review [æ] and [ə] and [ɑ]. Pronounce the following words, remembering that [æ] is tense, [ə] is lax, and [ɑ] is tense.

bag – bug – bog	pat – putt – pot
bam – bum – bomb	rat – rut – rot
cad – cud – cod	lack – luck – lock
cap – cup – cop	ma'am – mum – mom
cat – cut – cot	sack – suck – sock
gnat – nut – knot	tack – tuck – tock
hat – hut – hot	tags – tugs – togs
jag – jug – jog	

EXERCISE 76 Practice the following, applying the principles previously discussed.

1. Ireland has a lot of peat bogs.
2. Do you like codfish cakes?
3. You'll have to sleep on a cot tonight.
4. He bought a jug of wine.
5. Thank you, ma'am.
6. Are you afraid of rats?
7. Tuck in your shirt.
8. Could I bum a cigaret from you?
9. I've just had a cup of coffee.
10. Do you like candy with nuts in it?
11. My luck's been bad lately.
12. Don't pat me on the head.
13. You've got a hole in your sock.
14. You'd better put some tags on your bags.

REVIEW: DIALOGS 46-50

46. 1 – What do you like best in the world?
    2 – Sleep.
    1 – But you can't do anything while you're asleep.
    2 – That's why I like it.

47. 1 – What're you taking this semester?
    2 – Physics, history, chemistry, and math.
    1 – What's your hardest course?
    2 – Oh, history.
       I have to read a lot.

48. 1 – You look sick.
       What's the matter?
    2 – I've got a headache.
    1 – Maybe you're catching a cold.
    2 – I hope not.

49. 1 – I'm ready to give up.
    2 – What's the matter?
    1 – People talk too fast.
    2 – Would you mind speaking a little slower?
       I didn't understand you.

50. 1— May I speak to Mr. Brown, please?
    2— Who's calling, please?
    1— Tell him it's Robert King.
    2— Yes, sir.
        Just a moment, please.

REVIEW: QUOTATIONS 33-34

33. "Give me a theme," the little poet cried,
    "And I will do my part."
    "It's not a theme you need," the world replied;
    "You need a heart."

    — *Gilder*

34. Lives of great men all remind us
    We can make our lives sublime
    And, departing, leave behind us
    Footprints on the sands of time.

    — *Longfellow*

LESSON 31   Group Stress: Auxiliaries

An auxiliary is usually not stressed when it precedes a verb.
These words are often auxiliaries:

am	was	being	does	has	could	must	should
is	were	been	did	had	may	ought	will
are	be	do	have	can	might	shall	would

Unstressed *am* is usually reduced to $[m]$; *are*, to $[ə]$; *will* and
and *shall*, to $[l]$; *had* and *would* to $[d]$.

Unstressed *have* is reduced to $[v]$ after vowels and to $[əv]$ after
consonants.

Is and *has* are reduced to $[s]$ after voiceless sounds and to $[z]$
after voiced sounds. After a sibilant ($[s, z, ʃ, ʒ, tʃ, dʒ]$), unstressed
is is pronounced $[ɪz]$, and unstressed *has* is pronounced $[əz]$.

If an auxiliary is the last word in a sentence, it receives stress.
That auxiliary may have *-n't* with it. *Ought* is usually followed by
unstressed *to*.

All those reductions are customary in ordinary conversation even though in most writing the full forms *am, is,* etc., are used. Personal letters and dialogs frequently have the following contractions as representations of the reduced forms: *'s* for *is* or *has; 'm* for *am, 're* for *are; 'll* for *will* or *shall; 'd* for *had* or *would; 've* for *have.* Those contractions usually come after the personal pronouns, *there,* and the *wh* words *who, where,* etc.

EXERCISE 77 Pronounce the following sentences, stressing the verbs that come after the auxiliaries.

1. He was leaving.
2. They were coming.
3. The house is being painted.
4. Do you like it?
5. Did they win?
6. Are they sleeping?
7. They could answer.
8. He might leave.
9. The dish is broken.
10. He must be sleeping.
11. The class has been interesting.
12. Does he try?
13. Is he going?
14. She can sing.
15. You may go.
16. You should try it.

EXERCISE 78 Pronounce the following sentences with unstressed auxiliaries.

1. She is coming.
2. I am waiting.
3. He has seen her.
4. I would ask him.
5. The clock is running.
6. We are tired.
7. Mary will tell him.
8. The man has gone.
9. The men have gone.
10. The boy had finished.
11. The bus is crowded.
12. The judge has left.

EXERCISE 79 Add -*n't* to the full form of the first auxiliary in all the sentences in Exercises 77 and 78, for instance, "He wasn't leaving" and "She isn't coming." After *am* [m], add *not,* but don't stress it. Instead of *will not,* say *won't.* Don't stress any of the auxiliaries or the -*n't.* Don't pronounce the first *t* in *mustn't.*

EXERCISE 80 Pronounce the following sentences, and stress the final auxiliary.

1. I think I can.
2. I would go if I could.
3. I wish you wouldn't.
4. He thought he could.
5. He will do it if you think he ought to.
6. She doesn't want to go, but she will.
7. I am going because I must.
8. I hope you won't.
9. See me when you can.
10. They say they are tired, but they aren't.

LESSON 32 Question Tags

The auxiliaries are used in "question tags." To a statement are added the appropriate auxiliary and the personal pronoun equivalent of the subject. If the statement is positive, the auxiliary has -*n't* (except *am*); if the statement is negative, the auxiliary does not have -*n't*.

1. John likes Mary, doesn't he?
2. John doesn't like Mary, does he?

The intonation of the sentence depends on the intention of the speaker. Most often he is unsure about the statement and is asking for the opinion of his listener. He pauses slightly after the statement (Intonation Pattern 3) and then has rising intonation on the question tag (Intonation Pattern 2).

1. This is the right class, isn't it?
2. You didn't mean that, did you?

However, if the speaker is quite sure about the statement, he pauses after the statement (Intonation Pattern 3) and then has rising-falling intonation on the question tag (Intonation Pattern 1).

1. You didn't study, did you?
2. Most people try hard, don't they?

EXERCISE 81 Say the following sentences with rising intonation on the question tag.

1. He was leaving, wasn't he?
2. They weren't coming, were they?
3. The men could answer, couldn't they?
4. The dish isn't broken, is it?
5. He might leave, mightn't he?
6. She isn't coming, is she?
7. Mary will tell him, won't she?
8. The men haven't gone, have they?
9. The boy won, didn't he?
10. The girls like him, don't they?

EXERCISE 82 Repeat the sentences in Exercise 81 with rising-falling intonation.

LESSON 33 Tongue Between the Teeth

Put the tip of your tongue between your teeth for [ð] and [θ]. Don't stop the breath from coming out through your mouth, not even for a moment.   [ð] is **voiced**: the vocal cords vibrate; make the sound with little force.   [θ] is **voiceless**: the vocal cords do not vibrate; make the sound with much force.

EXERCISE 83 Pronounce the following words with [θ] and [ð]. The first word of each pair has [θ], and the second word has [ð].

thigh — thy   ether — either   loath — loathe
                                          sheath — sheathe
                                          teeth — teethe
                                          wreath — wreathe

EXERCISE 84 Practice the following, applying the principles previously discussed.

1. Did they give you ether when you had your operation?
2. The Bible says, "Honor thy father and thy mother."
3. I loathe liver.
4. He pulled the sword out of its sheath.
5. Babies cry a lot when they teethe, don't they?
6. She put a Christmas wreath on the front door.

LESSON 34 Two-Syllable Words: Stress on Second Syllable

The following words have stress on the second syllable. When you pronounce them, be sure to lengthen the stressed vowel.

1. [i]   compete, complete, deceive, decrease (v), defeat, degree
2. [ɪ]   dismiss, exist, forbid, forgive
3. [e]   behave, complain, contain, decay, delay
4. [ɛ]   defense, depend, descend, descent, despair, direct, effect, elect, event, except, expect, expense, express, extend
5. [æ]   attract, canal
6. [ə]   become, discuss
7. [ɑ]   beyond, forgot
8. [ɔ]   afford, along, applaud
9. [o]   below, compose, control
11. [u]   confuse, excuse, improve
12. [ɝ]   desert (v), deserve, disturb
13. [aɪ]   aside, behind, beside, combine, decide, delight, describe, desire
14. [aʊ]   allow, aloud, amount
15. [ɔɪ]   avoid, destroy

EXERCISE 85   Practice the following, applying the principles previously discussed.

1. I forgot to bring my book.
2. Who's sitting beside you?
3. We're going to dismiss classes early today.
4. Your teeth will decay if you don't brush them.
5. In any event, you ought to come to class.
6. You must control your temper.
7. Where's the Panama Canal?
8. That's no excuse.
9. He takes great delight in teasing his wife.
10. You didn't complete your assignment.
11. You should try to avoid making a mistake.
12. Are you working for a degree?
13. Do it without delay.
14. I can't afford to buy that.
15. Did Beethoven compose that piece?
16. She's in despair about her son.

17. A husband isn't supposed to desert his family.
18. Please read it aloud.
19. We'll discuss that later.
20. You'll deserve what you get, won't you?

EXERCISE 86 Practice pronouncing the following words with [t] and [s] and [θ] and [ʃ] and [tʃ]. Stop your breath for [t]. Don't stop your breath for [s], [θ], or [ʃ]. The position of the tip of your tongue distinguishes the four sounds. For [t], put the tip on your tooth ridge. For [s], put the tip close to your upper teeth, but don't touch them. For [θ], put the tip between your teeth lightly, but don't stop your breath. For [ʃ], put the tip close to your lower teeth, and protrude your lips. The sound [tʃ] is a combination of [t] and [ʃ]: put your tip on your tooth ridge and quickly move it down. All five sounds are voiceless: make them with much force.

> tin – sin – thin – shin – chin
> bat – bass – bath – bash – batch
> mat – mass – math – mash – match
> tie – sigh – thigh – shy
> tank – sank – thank – shank
> taw – saw – thaw – Shaw

EXERCISE 87 Practice the following, applying the principles previously discussed.

1. Have you read any of Shaw's plays?
2. The baby has a bruise on his thigh.
3. She sank into the chair with a sigh.
4. Stand on the bath mat when you get out of the shower.
5. The child thanked his father for the toy tank.
6. It's a shame the ice is too thin for skating.
7. This soup's too thin, isn't it?
8. You've got a spot on your tie.
9. That tenor starts singing in the shank of the evening.
10. The sailors had to lash the sail during the storm.
11. She put the frozen peas in the sink to let them thaw.
12. The bashful boy looked shyly at the teacher.
13. I'll be thankful when I can take a bath.
14. They sighed when they saw the ship sink without a sound.

EXERCISE 88 Review [ə] and [ɑ] and [ɔ]. Pronounce the following words, remembering that [ə] is lax, [ɑ] is tense, and [ɔ] is lax.

cud – cod – cawed
done – doń – dawn
tuck – tock – talk
tut – tot – taught
cut – cot – caught
huck – hock – hawk

nut – knot – naught
rut – rot – wrought
chuck – chock – chalk
fund – fond – fawned
stuck – stock – stalk

EXERCISE 89 Practice the following, applying the principles previously discussed.

1. They left at dawn this morning.
2. A clock goes "tick-tock."
3. He caught a cold from sitting in a draft.
4. He's very fond of children.
5. The clerk said the book was out of stock.
6. Have you ever watched a cow chew her cud?
7. Have you ever heard of King Tut?
8. He's going to hock his watch to get some money.
9. He doesn't want a job that'll get him in a rut, does he?

REVIEW: DIALOGS 51-55

51. 1 – What's that?
    2 – It's a tool chest.
    1 – What's it for?
    2 – To carry tools.

52. 1 – Where have you been?
       I haven't seen you for a long time.
    2 – I've been pretty busy.
       I've had a lot of work to do.
    1 – Everyone's missed you.
    2 – It's nice of you to say so.

53. 1 – Please give me two four-cent stamps.
       I'd also like three postcards.
    2 – That'll be twenty-three cents.
    1 – Do you have any airmail envelopes?
    2 – No, you'll have to get them in a store.

REVIEW: DIALOGS (Continued)

54. 1 — I can't hear the radio.
       Won't you turn it up?
    2 — The neighbors will complain if I do.
       Why don't you sit closer?
    1 — I'm right beside it now.
       I can't get any closer.

55. 1 — Did you have a good weekend?
    2 — Yes, I did.
    1 — What did you do?
    2 — I stayed at home and studied.

REVIEW: QUOTATIONS 35-36

35. It's good to be merry and wise;
    It's good to be honest and true.
    It's well to be off with the old love
    Before you go on with the new.

    — *Anonymous*

36. Work — work — work
       Till the brain begins to swim;
    Work — work — work
       Till the eyes are heavy and dim.

    — *Hood*

LESSON 35 Group Stress: Prepositions

Prepositions that precede their objects are usually not stressed. Words that are frequently prepositions are the following:

about	around	between	for	on	under
above	at	by	from	out	until
across	before	concerning	in	over	up
after	behind	despite	into	since	upon
against	below	down	like	till	with
along	beside	during	of	to	within
among	besides	except	off	toward	without

Be very careful about the pronunciation of the word *of:* it's almost always unstressed [əv].

LESSON 35   (Continued)

The usual pronunciation of *toward* is [tɔrd].

When *with* is followed by the word *the*, the two words have only one *th* sound: [wɪðə]; in ordinary speech, *with the* and *with a* sound alike.

EXERCISE 90   Say the three words in the following list as a "breath group": don't pause between the words, and stress only the noun. Be sure to lengthen the stressed vowel of the noun:

at my bank	after an hour	around the window
with the doctor	against their car	besides his family
in her town	despite her conduct	of your house
since our party	without his mother	for a time
up a river	along its edge	out a dollar
under the earth	below a table	toward the light
between my sons	like a friend	over your head
within a week	down his street	beside a fire
across an ocean	on the wall	into the city
behind the school	to the person	above the picture
from the child	during the night	before your eyes
by a road	among the people	until the evening
off a tree	except his room	concerning a man
till a morning	about its result	upon my honor

LESSON 36   Distinguishing [ɚ] and Vowel + [r]

To make the vowel [ɚ] and the consonant [r], you do the same thing: you put the tip of your tongue near the tooth ridge and bend the tip backward.

Don't touch anything, and don't shake anything.

Make the sound [n] — touch your tooth ridge with the tip of your tongue; then make [ɚ] — move the tip backward. Then say the sounds one after the other: [n ... ɚ ... n ... ɚ]. Then say [d ... ɚ ... d ... ɚ] and [t ... ɚ ... t ... ɚ]. Finally, say [l ... ɚ ... l ... ɚ]. Then pronounce the words *nerve* [nɚv], *dirt* [dɚt], *turn* [tɚn], and *learn* [lɚn].

Don't let the tip shake when you make [r]: hold the tip back firmly — you can with practice. Pronounce *car* [kar], *here* [hɪr], and *war* [wɔr].

66

LESSON 36 (Continued)

Don't let your uvula shake. Your uvula is that thing that hangs down in the back of your mouth; you can see it in a mirror. Bend your head far back, and say [r]; then with your head in its natural position, say [r]. If you hear a difference, you probably let your uvula vibrate with the second [r]. Pronounce [ɑ] and then [r]. Your breath should come out of your mouth in the same way; there should be no "rubbing" sound accompanying the [r].

The symbol [ɚ] represents one sound, and the symbol [r] represents one sound. In the word *fur* there are two sounds: [f] and [ɚ]. In the word *far* there are three sounds: [f] and [ɑ] and [r]. In each word in the first column of the following list, the letter *r* and the vowel letter or letters preceding it represent just one sound: [ɚ]. In the other columns, the vowel letter or letters before the *r* represent one sound, and the following *r* represents a separate sound. Two *r* letters together are pronounced just like a single *r*.

You will hear differences among native speakers in their pronunciation of stressed vowels before [r]. For example, for *beard* some people say [bɪrd], and others say [bɪrd]. For *care* some say [kɛr], others [kær], and still others [ker]. For *board* some say [bord], and others [bɔrd]. For *boor* some say [bur], and others [bʊr].

EXERCISE 91 Practice the following, applying the principles previously discussed.

[ɚ]	[ɪr]	[ɛr]	[ɑr]	[ɔr]	[ʊr]
bird	beard	bared	barred	board	–
burn	–	–	barn	born	–
burr	beer	bear	bar	bore	boor
cur	–	care	car	core	–
curse	–	–	–	course	–
curd	–	cared	card	cord	–
curt	–	–	cart	court	–
dirt	–	–	dart	–	–
err	ear	air	are	or	–
firm	–	–	farm	form	–
fur	fear	fair	far	four	–
gird	geared	–	guard	gourd	–
heard	–	haired	hard	hoard	–
hearse	–	–	–	horse	–
her	hear	hair	–	–	–

EXERCISE 92 Practice the following, applying the principles previously discussed.

1. Do you like a man with a beard?
2. The farmer wanted to burn the barn.
3. Would you like a glass of beer?
4. That happened before you were born.
5. Most flowers grow in dirt.
6. Don't curse this course; be patient.
7. I had an ear of corn at lunch.
8. How much do you pay for room and board?
9. He ate the apple and threw away the core.
10. He finally bared his secret, didn't he?
11. I heard what you said.
12. A boor is a bore.
13. It isn't nice to call a man a cur.
14. Does a bear have fur?
15. To err is human; to forgive, divine.
16. Horses used to draw hearses.
17. Pull the cord when you want to get off.
18. A clerk shouldn't be curt to customers, should he?

LESSON 37   Group Stress: Personal Pronouns

The pronouns *I, me, we, us, you, he, him, she, her, it, they,* and *them* are usually not stressed.

The *h* in the words *he, him,* and *her* is customarily not pronounced unless those words begin a sentence.

Unstressed *me* is pronounced [mɪ].

EXERCISE 93 Practice saying the following sentence without stressing the pronouns:

1. I saw him.
2. We knew her.
3. They left me.
4. She asked them.
5. We want it.
6. Tell him you like him.
7. Tell her you love her.
8. You need them.

9. He told me.
10. I wrote it.
11. She took us.
12. They paid her.
13. Phone me if you need me.
14. Don't tell him where we're going.

REVIEW: DIALOGS 56-60

56. 1 — What does that sign say?
    2 — Can't you read it?
    1 — No, I can't.
    Please tell me what it says.
    2 — It says "No Smoking."
    You'd better put out your cigaret.

57. 1 — What were you doing at the store yesterday?
    2 — I was looking for a spring suit.
    What were you doing there?
    1 — I was trying to find a coat.
    I need a light one for bad weather.

58. 1 — We're going to the park.
    Would you like to come along?
    2 — I'd like to, but I've got to do some shopping.

59. 1 — Can you go with us tomorrow?
    2 — Yes, I can.
    I can borrow some money to go.
    1 — Why couldn't you go last week?
    2 — Because I couldn't borrow any money.

60. 1 — Where's Fred?
    What's he doing?
    2 — He's out in the driveway.
    He's washing the car.
    1 — Does he need any help?
    2 — I don't think so.

37. What are little girls made off?
Sugar and spice and all that's nice.
What are little boys made of?
Snakes and snails and puppy-dog tails.

— *Anonymous*

38. Sweet and low, sweet and low,
Wind of the western sea.
Low, low, breathe and blow,
Wind of the western sea.

— *Tennyson*

LESSON 38 Group Stress: Prepositions and Pronouns

When a preposition is followed by a personal pronoun as its object, the preposition is usuallv stressed, but the pronoun is not.

When *with* and *them* come together, there is only one *th* sound: ['wɪðəm].

EXERCISE 94 Practice combining a prepositior and a pronoun, stressing only the preposition. Say the sentence "He came with us," and then substitute other prepositions such as *by, for, after, before, between, beside, across,* and *behind* for the *with.* Then, substitute for *us* the other personal pronouns *me, you, him, her, it,* and *them.*

EXERCISE 95 Review [ɑ] and [ɔ] and [o]. Pronounce the following words, remembering that [ɑ] is tense, [ɔ] is lax, and [o] is tense.

chock — chalk — choke	rah — raw — row
cod — cawed — code	rot — wrought — wrote
cot — caught — coat	sod — sawed — sewed
fond — fawned — phoned	stock — stalk — stoke
knot — naught — note	tot — taught — tote
,nod — gnawed — node	

EXERCISE 96 Practice the following, applying the principles previously discussed.

1. Do you know the Morse code?
2. He caught the train just as it was leaving.
3. Did you get my note?
4. You shouldn't eat raw pork.
5. Would you like to stoke a furnace on a ship?
6. That was a huge dinner; I'm chock-full.
7. I phoned you last night, but you weren't in.
8. The dog gnawed the bone.
9. Dead trees gradually rot away.
10. He's taught English for a number of years.

LESSON 39　The Sounds [j] and [dʒ]

The sound [j] occurs only before a vowel. It is usually spelled *y*, as in *yellow* and *yet*, but it also is frequently part of the sounds represented by the letter *u*, as in *unite* and *particular*.

The easiest way to make [j] is to pronounce it as though it were unstressed [i] before another vowel. Practice these combinations, putting extra stress on the second vowel: [ie], [iɑ], [io], and [iu]. You can do the same with [ii]: try *yeast* and *yield*.

If you have trouble distinguishing [j] and [dʒ], do this: put the tip of your tongue lightly against your *lower* front teeth when you begin to make [j]. For [dʒ], begin by pressing the tip of your tongue firmly against your *upper* tooth ridge.

EXERCISE 97 Practice the following, applying the principles previously discussed.

Yale — jail	yet — jet
yam — jam	yoke — joke
yard — jarred	you — Jew
year — jeer	use (verb) — Jews
yellow — Jello	use (noun) — juice
yell — jell	

71

EXERCISE 98 Practice the following, applying the principles previously discussed.

1. He's going to Yale.
2. The earthquake jarred the house.
3. Don't yell; I can hear you.
4. He hasn't seen a jet yet, has he?
5. Carrying a yoke is no joke.
6. Do Jews use that synagogue?
7. Do you like jam?
8. The crowd jeered the umpire.
9. Lemon Jello is yellow.
10. Are you a Jew?
11. He has no use for juice.

EXERCISE 99 Practice the following, applying the principles previously discussed.

east — yeast	earn — yearn
ale — Yale	s — yes
am — yam	oak — yoke
ear — year	l (the letter) — yell

EXERCISE 100 Practice the following, applying the principles previously discussed.

1. Yeast is used in making bread.
2. Are you as fond of yams as I am?
3. Don't yearn for what you haven't got.
4. The word yes has an s at the end.
5. Do you like oak furniture?
6. Can you drink ale at Yale?
7. His ear has been bothering him for a year, hasn't it?
8. There are two l's in yell.

EXERCISE 101 Review group stress. Stress the noun: lengthen the stressed vowel. Don't stop between the words of the group.

of school	a cold	a theory
of course	your homework	in the world
the matter	to school	the catch
a headache	a lot	to the radio
at Macy's	of things	my parents
of money	the kind	to a lot

LESSON 40   Group Stress: Conjunctions

Conjunctions are usually not stressed. These words may be conjunctions:

after	as	but	nor	than	till
although	because	for	or	that	until
and	before	if	since	though	while

In ordinary speech, *and* is often reduced to [n], and *or* is reduced to [ə].

EXERCISE 102   Practice the following groups. Don't stop after the conjunctions, and don't stress them.

1. a boy and a man
2. the girl or the woman
3. He's as good as the man.
4. He's better than the man.
5. if you can
6. I told him that I could.
7. after we took it
8. for they need it
9. till we were tired
10. as you know
11. before he left
12. although he shouldn't
13. because he saw her
14. but I can't
15. neither John nor Mary
16. while you were studying
17. before the train arrived
18. since I came here
19. until the accident happened
20. as I told you

EXERCISE 103 Review [ɔ] and [o] and [ʊ]. Pronounce the following words, remembering that [ɔ] is lax, [o] is tense, and [ʊ] is lax.

> ball – bowl – bull
> hawks – hoax – hooks
> Paul – pole – pull
> calk – coke – cook
> cawed – code – could
> fall – foal – full

EXERCISE 104 Practice the following, applying the principles previously discussed.

1. You'll have to pull the window down with that pole.
2. Will you be here next fall?
3. She drank a Coke with her sandwich.
4. The crow cawed and flew away.
5. I wish I could cook like Paul.
6. The maid sought to clean all the bowls.
7. The salesman who sold hooks was responsible for the hoax.
8. You should have showed us some good books.
9. She put the ball of wool on a hook on the wall.

REVIEW: DIALOGS 61-65

61. 1 – What does "Take it easy" mean?
    2 – "Relax" or "Don't rush."
    1 – Does it always mean that?
    2 – No. It sometimes means "Goodby."

62. 1 – Do you know who Romeo and Juliet were?
    2 – Of course I do.
    They were the greatest lovers in the world.
    1 – That's just a fairy tale.
    2 – You're a cynic.

63. 1 – Where were you last week?
    2 – In Washington.
    1 – Why did you go?
    2 – We went to visit my wife's family.

64. 1 — Pardon me.
     Would you help me, please?
   2 — I'll try.
   1 — How do I get to the Registrar's Office?
   2 — Do you see that building with the round top?
     It's in the large building behind it.

65. 1 — Didn't Arthur finish the work?
   2 — I don't think so.
   1 — Does he expect us to finish it?
   2 — I hope not.
     I certainly don't intend to.

REVIEW: QUOTATIONS 39-40

39. Hope is the thing with feathers
    That perches in the soul
    And sings the tune without the words
    And never stops at all.

    — *Dickinson*

40. We may live without poetry, music, and art;
    We may live without conscience and live without heart;
    We may live without friends; we may live without books;
    But civilized man can not live without cooks.

    — *Meredith*

LESSON 41   Syllabic [n] and [l]

A number of words have an unstressed syllable that is pronounced without a vowel. The syllable begins with [d] or [t] and ends in [n] or [l]. Such a syllable has a "syllabic *n*" or a "syllabic *l.*"

To make a syllabic [n], put your tongue tip on your tooth ridge for the *d* or *t* and leave it there while you let your breath out through your nose. Don't move your tongue before you start the [n]; if you do, you will probably make an [ə] sound. Don't stress the [n] syllable; stress the preceding syllable.

LESSON 41 (Continued)

To make a syllabic [l], put your tongue tip on your tooth ridge for the [d] or [t], and leave it there while you pronounce the [l] by letting your breath come over the sides of your tongue.

EXERCISE 105 Pronounce the following words without moving your tongue after you have put it on your tooth ridge for the [d] or [t].

curtain	eaten	brighten	little
Latin	sudden	forgotten	idle
satin	sadden	Britain	cattle

EXERCISE 106 You can add other sounds after a syllabic [n]. Add [lɪ] to *certain* and *sudden:* say [ˈsɚtnlɪ] and [ˈsədnlɪ]. Don't move your tongue between the [t] or [d] and the [n]. Now say the following sentences:

1. That was certainly all right.   2. He left very suddenly.

EXERCISE 107 Add [z] to these words:

curtain	pardon	widen	kitten	idol
broaden	button	sadden	brighten	battle
garden	harden	mitten	frighten	cradle

EXERCISE 108 Practice the following, applying the principles previously discussed.

1. The living room has new curtains.
2. The garden's very pretty.
3. You stepped on the little kitten's tail
4. Did you find the buttons and the mittens?
5. The avenue widens in the middle of Thirtieth Street.

EXERCISE 109 Add [d] to these words:

broaden	harden	tighten	bottle
pardon	widen	heighten	fiddle
button	sadden	brighten	settle

76

EXERCISE 110 Practice the following, applying the principles previously discussed.

1. You certainly frightened me.
2. He threatened to resign.
3. John buttoned his shirt.
4. The cook ladled the noodles into the bowl.
5. He straightened his necktie.
6. Third Avenue has been widened.
7. She suddenly hardened her heart and settled in her chair.
8. He tightened his belt.

EXERCISE 111 The contraction -*n't* is pronounced with a syllabic [n] in *didn't, wouldn't, couldn't,* and *shouldn't.* Say the following sentences, but don't explode the final [t] violently.

1. I didn't ask him.
2. They couldn't help me.
3. She wouldn't leave.
4. You shouldn't eat that.

EXERCISE 112 The word *important* also has a syllabic [n]. Say the following sentences:

1. It's an important message.
2. He acts like an important person.

EXERCISE 113 The word *and* is frequently pronounced as a syllabic [n]. Practice it in these sentences:

1. I want some bread and butter.
2. He worked hard and long.
3. They gave him food and drink.
4. He tried and succeeded.
5. The preacher talked about David and Goliath.
6. She spends my money right and left.
7. He likes meat and potatoes.
8. Read the first and second pages.
9. He put his heart and soul into the project.
10. He fought and won.
11. The baby was tired and sleepy.
12. He worries night and day.
13. The day was wet and cold.
14. Dad and Mother are coming.

LESSON 42 Three-Syllable Words: Stress on First Syllable

The following words have stress on the first syllable. When you pronounce them, be sure to lengthen the stressed vowel.

1. [i] equally, frequently
2. [ɪ] imitate, indicate, industry, influence, instantly, instrument, interested
3. [e] hastily
4. [ɛ] excellent, exercise, generally, gentleman, hesitate, jealousy, medicine, medical, membership, messenger, prejudice, president, recognize, regular
5. [æ] capital, character, classify, handkerchief, management, manager, national, naturally
6. [ə] governor, multiply, otherwise, punishment
7. [ɑ] holiday, honorable, hospital, moderate, operate, opposite, policy, politics, popular
8. [ɔ] loyalty, orderly, organize
9. [o] notify
11. [u] musical, newspaper
12. [ɚ] furniture, perfectly
13. [aɪ] quietly, scientist
14. [aʊ] powerful

EXERCISE 114 Practice the following, applying the principles previously discussed.

1. He frequently stays out all night.
2. A dentist has a lot of instruments.
3. He hastily apologized when he saw I was angry.
4. Rabbits multiply rapidly, don't they?
5. When's the doctor going to operate?
6. Notify me when you're ready.
7. He's planning to be a scientist.
8. Imitate your teacher as closely as you can.
9. No gentleman would say that, would he?
10. Complain to the manager if the service is poor.
11. He has an orderly mind.
12. I saw it in the newspaper.
13. He has powerful hands.

LESSON 43   The Sound [h]

The sound [h] occurs only before a vowel or [j] or [w]. The letter *h* at the beginning of a word or syllable is usually pronounced. The major exceptions are *hour, honor, heir, exhibit,* and *exhaust* and their derivatives. The *h* is usually not pronounced in *he, his, him,* and *her* unless those words begin a sentence or are emphasized. Remember that the unstressed auxiliaries *have, has,* and *had* are usually reduced to [v], [z] or [s], and [d]. Don't try to pronounce the *h* in words like *John, Sarah,* and *Utah.*

The combination [hw], spelled *wh,* as in *white, why, what, while,* and *when,* is frequently reduced to [w], particularly if the word in which it occurs is not stressed. If you stress the word, you had better pronounce the full combination. Don't forget that *who, whose, whom,* and *whole* don't have any [w] sound: [hu], [huz], [hum], [hol].

If you have trouble making the English [h], try whispering. Start by whispering a vowel and then continue the vowel in your natural voice. Practice with [o]: [h ... o]. However, don't make a rustling sound in the back of your mouth or throat.

EXERCISE 115   Practice saying these pairs:

ear – hear	*l* (the letter) – hell	arm – harm
eat – heat	ate – hate	art – heart
ill – hill	it – hit	ash – hash
am – ham	I – high	*A* – hey
old – hold	all – hall	Ellen – Helen
	air – hair	

EXERCISE 116   Practice the following, applying the principles previously discussed.

1. We hear with our ears.
2. Do you like to climb high hills?
3. Hey, how are you?
4. What did he say?
5. He hit the boy in the hall.
6. You'd better behave.
7. The huge whale was white.
8. He's an honorable man.
9. I like Ellen, but not Helen.

10. Did it hurt?
11. There are two *l*'s in *hell*.
12. You can have hash or ham and eggs.
13. You go ahead; I'll be with you in an hour.
14. The heat in summer can make you feel ill, can't it?
15. The heir received a hundred thousand dollars.
16. Who could be happier than John?
17. Does hot water harm your hair?

EXERCISE 117 Review [o] and [ʊ] and [u]. Pronounce the following words, remembering that [o] is tense, [ʊ] is lax, and [u] is tense.

code – could – cooed   foal – full – fool
stowed – stood – stewed   pole – pull – pool
hoed – hood – who'd   showed – should – shoed

EXERCISE 118 Practice the following, applying the principles previously discussed.

1. Did that trick fool you?
2. Please pull the shade down.
3. Do you always do what you should?
4. Let's go swimming in the pool.
5. I wish I could, but I can't.
6. The pigeons cooed after they'd eaten.
7. He showed me how to do it.
8. Life is full of surprises, isn't it?
9. The mare acts proud of her foal.
10. That vine will climb up a pole.

REVIEW: DIALOGS 66-70

66. 1 – Do women wear veils very often?
    2 – Not nowadays.
    1 – I bet they don't want to hide their beauty.
    2 – Well, we're all very vain, you know.

67. 1 — How much are your bananas, sir?
    2 — Twenty-five cents a pound, ma'am.
    1 — All right. I'll take two pounds.
    2 — Anything else?
    1 — No, thank you.

68. 1 — Are you working for a degree?
    2 — Yes, I am.
    1 — Which one?
    2 — M.A.
    1 — In which field?
    2 — Philosophy.

69. 1 — When's the next leap year?
    2 — Next year, isn't it?
    1 — Will February have twenty-eight days or twenty-nine?
    2 — Twenty-eight.

70. 1 — Do you like this kind of weather?
    2 — Oh, no, I don't.
    1 — Is it better in your country?
    2 — Oh, no. It's worse.

REVIEW: QUOTATIONS 41-42

41. I know some poison I could drink;
        I've often thought I'd taste it;
    But Mother bought it for the sink,
        And drinking it would waste it.
                — *Millay*

42. She walks in beauty, like the night
        Of cloudless climes and starry skies,
    And all that's best of dark and bright
        Meet in her aspect and her eyes.
                — *Byron*

There are a few times when you can be sure that certain letters are not pronounced. Those times are the following:

b after **m** at the end of a word: bomb, climb, comb, crumb, dumb, lamb, limb, numb, thumb.

g before **n** at the beginning of a word: gnash, gnat, gnaw, gnome.
before **n** at the end of a word: campaign, design, foreign, sign.
before **m** at the end of a word: diaphragm, paradigm, phlegm.

gh before **t** at the end of a word: night, light, caught, bought.

h after **g** at the beginning of a word: ghetto, ghost, ghoul.
after **r** at the beginning of a word: rhetoric, rhinoceros, rhubarb, rhythm.
after **ex** at the beginning of a word: exhibit, exhaust, exhilarate, exhort.
at the end of a word: ah, catarrh, myrrh, Sarah, Utah.

k before **n** at the beginning of a word: knee, knife, knock, know.

l in the combination **alf** at the end of a word: calf, half.
in the combination **alk** at the end of a word: chalk, stalk, talk, walk.
in the combination **alm** at the end of a word: calm, palm.

m before **n** at the beginning of a word: mnemonic, Mnemosyne.

n after **m** at the end of a word: autumn, column, hymn, solemn.

p before **n** at the beginning of a word: pneumatic, pneumonia.
before **s** at the beginning of a word: psalm, pseudonym, psychic, psychology.
before **t** at the beginning of a word: ptomaine, Ptolemy.

t in the combination **sten** at the end of a word: fasten, hasten, listen.
in the combination **stle** at the end of a word: apostle, castle, whistle.

w before **r** at the beginning of a word: wrap, wreck, write, wrong.

EXERCISE 119 Practice the following, applying the principles previously discussed.

1. Listen to what I tell you.
2. I want half of that.
3. There's some chalk by the blackboard.
4. A mnemonic aid helps you remember.
5. Have you ever had pneumonia?
6. Your thumb is on your hand.
7. Utah is one of the States.
8. Dogs gnaw bones, don't they?
9. Your diaphragm helps you breathe.
10. I caught a cold yesterday.
11. Do you like ghost stories?
12. Listen to the rhythm of the sentence.
13. She's going to study psychology.
14. Peter was an apostle, wasn't he?
15. That's a pretty design.
16. He's a very calm person.
17. The congregation sang a hymn in church.
18. He saw the exhibit in the museum.
19. Have you ever eaten rhubarb pie?
20. You can get ptomaine poisoning from spoiled food.
21. The clerk will wrap the package.
22. Children like to climb trees.
23. My foot feels numb.
24. He had a lamb chop for dinner.
25. Can you guess what happened?
26. There was a bad wreck on the highway.

EXERCISE 120 Review [d] and [ð]. Touch your tooth ridge for [d]; put your tongue tip between your teeth for [ð].

d's – these	ladder – lather	laid – lathe
day – they	reading – wreathing	reed – wreathe
die – thy	riding – writhing	ride – writhe
dough – though		sued – soothe
doze – those		

EXERCISE 121 Practice the following, applying the principles previously discussed.

1. These words have a lot of *d*'s.
2. Flowers die in the fall, don't they?
3. He laid it on the table.
4. He sued the company for ten thousand dollars.
5. Do they do that every day?
6. You mustn't doze in class.
7. A lot of musical horns have a reed in the mouth piece.

EXERCISE 122 Review [t] and [θ]. Touch your tooth ridge for [t]; put your tongue tip between your teeth for [θ].

tank — thank	trash — thrash	bat — bath
team — theme	tree — three	boot — booth
tie — thigh	true — through	fate — faith
		oat — oath

EXERCISE 123 Practice the following, applying the principles previously discussed.

1. Thanks a lot.
2. Do you like the thigh of a chicken?
3. There're three trees in a row.
4. She's taking a bath right now.
5. I don't have any faith in his promises.
6. Be sure to hand in your theme tomorrow.
7. Fathers used to thrash their boys; now they spank them.
8. Where's the nearest telephone booth?
9. Doctors take an oath when they graduate.

LESSON 45 Two-Syllable Words: Stress on First Syllable

The following words have stress on the first syllable. When you pronounce them, be sure to lengthen the stressed vowel.

1. [i] eastern, easy, either
2. [ɪ] city, clearly, clearness, children, critic, difference, different, dinner

3. [e] basis, cable, crazy, danger, dangerous
4. [ɛ] center, chairman, clever, desert (n), devil, effort, elder, elsewhere, empire, empty, endless
5. [æ] anger, angry, answer, apple, arrow, average, backward, badly
6. [ə] comfort, country, couple, cousin, cover, custom, double
7. [ɑ] bother, bottle, bottom, collar, college, conference, commerce
8. [ɔ] autumn, awful, awfully
9. [o] local, lonely, lower
10. [ʊ] during
11. [u] duty, foolish
12. [ɚ] curtain, dirty, early
13. [ɑɪ] final, Friday, highly
14. [ɑʊ] council
15. [ɔɪ] poison

EXERCISE 124 Practice the following, applying the principles previously discussed.

1. Do you think English is easy?
2. Everybody said the chairman was crazy.
3. His room was awfully dirty.
4. I don't like to bother you.
5. A country cousin is one who doesn't live in the city.
6. I shot an arrow into the air.
7. That's clearly dangerous.
8. Do your duty.
9. I don't get up early on Friday.
10. I can't see much difference between those two children.
11. It's foolish to drink poison, isn't it?
12. When you're lonely, you feel awful.
13. Her answer made him angry.
14. Are you going to the conference tomorrow?
15. It's a comfort to feel you're clever.
16. You can either go or stay.
17. That's a custom of the country.

LESSON 46 Homophones

There are groups of words which are spelled differently but are pronounced the same. Such words are called *homophones* or *homonyms*. Some of them are the following:

aisle – isle – I'll	cite – site – sight	rain – reign – rein
B – be – bee	flu – flew – flue	right – write – rite
C – see – sea	I – eye – aye	so – sew – sow
cent – sent – scent	pair – pear – pare	T – tea – tee

EXERCISE 125 Practice the following, applying the principles previously discussed.

1. I'll go with you.
2. Have you ever had flu?
3. When did Charlemagne reign?
4. Don't put your feet in the aisle.
5. A golfer knows what a tee is.
6. She was stung by a bee.
7. Smoke goes up a flue.
8. She ate a pear for dessert.
9. A small island is sometimes called an isle.
10. It won't cost you a cent, will it?
11. He flew to Georgia yesterday.
12. He got a *B* in the course, didn't he?
13. I need a new pair of shoes.
14. You'd better sew on that button.
15. A new building is going up on that site.
16. That rose has a sweet scent.
17. When you agree to a proposal, you say, "Aye."
18. "As you sow, so shall you reap."
19. A ceremony is sometimes referred to as a rite.
20. Do you want lemon with your tea?

EXERCISE 126 Review [ʃ] and [ʒ]. For both [ʃ] and [ʒ], put your tongue tip close to your lower teeth, and protrude your lips. Don't stop your breath. Make [ʃ] with much force; make [ʒ] with little force.

Aleutian – allusion
dilution – delusion
glacier – glazier

EXERCISE 127 Practice the following, applying the principles previously discussed.

1. The Aleutian Islands are off the coast of Alaska.
2. If you believe that, you're suffering from a delusion.
3. He made an allusion to the Holy Roman Empire.
4. The glazier will replace the window pane.

EXERCISE 128 Review [tʃ] and [dʒ]. For both [tʃ] and [dʒ], first stop your breath by putting your tongue tip on your tooth ridge, and then release your breath by moving the tip down quickly. Make [tʃ] with much force; make [dʒ] with little force.

chin – gin	chest – jest	batch – badge
char – jar	choke – joke	rich – ridge
cheer – jeer	chunk – junk	breeches – bridges
	chump – jump	

EXERCISE 129 Practice the following, applying the principles previously discussed.

1. The British drink a lot of gin.
2. If they like you, they'll cheer; if they don't, they'll jeer.
3. You mustn't call anybody a chump.
4. Put the tip of your tongue on your tooth ridge.
5. Do you want a jar of cherries?
6. The doctor examined the boy's chest.
7. Don't get mad; it was only a joke.
8. The detective showed his badge to the policeman.
9. How many bridges are there to cross?

EXERCISE 130 Review [i] and [ɪ] and [e]. Pronounce the following words, remembering that [i] is tense; [ɪ] is lax, and [e] is tense.

beat – bit – bait	meet – mitt – mate
ease – is – A's	peel – pill – pale
feel – fill – fail	reason – risen – raisin
heel – hill – hail	seen – sin – sane
lead – lid – laid	sleek – slick – slake
least – list – laced	

EXERCISE 131 Practice the following, applying the principles previously discussed.

1. Which team beat?
2. You'd better fill the gasoline tank before you start, hadn't you?
3. Lift the lid, and see if the pot's dry.
4. Let me help you peel the oranges.
5. I haven't seen him for two years.
6. This pill will ease the pain.
7. Did you get any *A*'s last term?
8. I've got to get new heels put on my shoes, haven't I?
9. Did you make out a laundry list?
10. I'll meet you at three.
11. Do you like raisin bread?
12. You need some new tires; your old ones are getting slick.

REVIEW: DIALOGS 71-75

71. 1 – Didn't you use to smoke?
    2 – Yes, I did.
    1 – What made you give it up?
    2 – My wife.

72. 1 – I've been working too hard.
    2 – You have?
    1 – Yes. Let's go to the theater tonight.
    2 – All right. Let's.

73. 1 – Do you like raw vegetables?
    2 – Yes, as a matter of fact, I do.
    1 – What kind do you like?
    2 – Oh, celery, lettuce, carrots – a lot of them.

74. 1 – I'm beginning to get worried.
    2 – Why, what's wrong?
    1 – I think I'm not going to pass this course.
    2 – Oh, well, while there's life, there's hope.

75. 1 – You've seen it hail, haven't you?
    2 – Oh, yes. It often hails in my country.
    1 – Does it ever snow?
    2 – Only in the mountains.

43. Amoebas at the start
Were not complex.
They tore themselves apart
And started sex.

— *Guiterman*

44. The night has a thousand eyes,
And the day but one;
Yet the light of the bright world dies
With the dying sun.

— *Bourdillon*

LESSON 47 Initial *s*

The letter *s* at the beginning of a word is nearly always pronounced voiceless [s]. The major exceptions are words beginning with *sh* and the words *sure* and *sugar*, all of which are pronounced with [ʃ]. Initial *sc* before the letters *e* and *i* is pronounced [s], but before other letters the combination is usually pronounced [sk].

Be sure to make initial [s] voiceless before a following consonant. Don't substitute [ʃ] or [z], and don't put an [ɛ] before the [s]. Practice making [s] alone and then adding the other consonant; for example, [s ... m] in *small, smoke, smile,* and [s ... l] in *slow, sleep, slang.*

EXERCISE 132 Practice the following, applying the principles previously discussed.

scale	sleep	snarl	stage
scarce	small	snatch	stairs
scarcely	smart	space	stamp
scatter	smash	spare	swallow
slang	smell	speak	swear
slap	snake	special	sweat
slave	snap	staff	Sweden

89

EXERCISE 133 Practice the following, applying the principles previously discussed.

1. Do you speak Spanish?
2. Horses are getting scarce.
3. The money was scattered over the floor.
4. Don't do that; she'll slap your face.
5. He promised his girl friend that he would be her slave.
6. That wasn't a smart thing to say.
7. Doesn't that smell good?
8. He snapped the light on.
9. The thief snatched her purse and ran.
10. Leave spaces on both sides of the paper.
11. She's a stage star.
12. Did you put enough stamps on that package?
13. You mustn't swear; it's not nice.
14. She comes from Sweden, doesn't she?
15. Can you sing a scale?
16. He can scarcely make himself understood, can he?
17. Are you beginning to pick up some slang?
18. How did you sleep last night?
19. Their baby is still quite small.
20. The ball smashed the window.
21. Are you afraid of snakes?
22. The dog will snarl if you try to take his food away.
23. He's a special friend of mine.
24. The office has a large staff.
25. He walked up the stairs very slowly.
26. Do you have any trouble swallowing pills?
27. The boys were sweating after the game.
28. Can you spare a dime?

LESSON 48 Three-Syllable Words: Stress on Second Syllable

The following words have stress on the second syllable. When you pronounce them, be sure to lengthen the stressed vowel.

1. [i] convenient, extremely, machinery
2. [ɪ] decision, deliver, delivery, description, distinguish, division, efficient, existence, familiar, musician
3. [e] container, courageous, occasion
4. [ɛ] effective, election, electric, essential, exception, excessive, expensive, expression, extension, extensive, however, intention, invention, inventor, objection
5. [æ] elastic, exactly, examine
6. [ə] discover, discovery, discussion, instruction
7. [ɑ] apartment, astonish, department
8. [ɔ] importance, important
9. [o] October
11. [u] confusion, improvement
12. [ə] determine
13. [aɪ] exciting, excitement
15. [ɔɪ] employee, employer

EXERCISE 134 Practice the following, applying the principles previously discussed.

1. Do you like to work with machinery?
2. Bring a container of milk when you come home.
3. Is your watch band elastic?
4. They took a vote without further discussion.
5. Will I see you in October?
6. Your work throughout the semester will determine your grade.
7. He's an employee of the bank on the corner.
8. After he makes a decision, he sticks to it.
9. If you have no objection, I'll turn the radio on.
10. Did you find a furnished apartment?
11. He attached no importance to what she said, did he?
12. Let's see if we can't straighten out the confusion.
13. The game was very exciting, wasn't it?
14. His employer was extremely astonished.

EXERCISE 135 Review group stress. Stress the noun: lengthen the stressed vowel. Don't stop between the words of the group.

the things	a foreigner	for breakfast
like eggs	to the theater	of shows
of courses	an airplane	on Sunday
my lessons	to church	a policeman
the names	of the days	for a week

EXERCISE 136 Review [s] and [ʃ]. For [s], put your tongue tip near your upper front teeth; for [ʃ], put your tongue tip near your lower front teeth. Don't stop your breath for either sound. Make both of them with much force.

same — shame	sore — shore	brass — brash
save — shave	sort — short	class — clash
séat — sheet	furnace — furnish	gas — gash
see — she	Paris — parish	lass — lash
sell — shell		mass — mash
so — show		mess — mesh
sock — shock		plus — plush
suit — shoot		Swiss — swish

EXERCISE 137 Practice the following, applying the principles previously discussed.

1. It's a shame you weren't with us last night, isn't it?
2. Could I borrow a sheet of paper?
3. Did she see you?
4. I hope that suits you.
5. Every time we try to discuss something, we have a clash.
6. His room's in a mess.
7. Five plus six equal eleven.
8. He picked up a shell on the shore.
9. Did you shave this morning?
10. I'll show you so you'll know how to do it.
11. Did you get a shock from the lamp?
12. That pipe's made of brass.
13. He cut a gash in his arm, didn't he?
14. He watched the waves lash the shore during the storm.
15. She likes silk dresses because they swish.

LESSON 49 *Have to* and *Has to*

The combination *have to* meaning "must" is customarily pronounced [ˈhæftə]. *Has to* with the same meaning is pronounced [ˈhæstə].

EXERCISE 138 Practice the following, applying the principles previously discussed.

1. I have to go now.
2. Do you have to tell me?
3. He has to walk a long way to school.
4. They let him stay because they have to.
5. We have to study very hard, don't we?
6. That tooth will have to come out.
7. Does he have to come to class tomorrow?
8. He sleeps only when he has to.

EXERCISE 139 Review the -*s* inflection. Add the sound [ɪz] to the following words:

advise	civilize	exchange	organize	push	touch
amuse	close	express	pass	realize	urge

EXERCISE 140 Review the -*s* inflection. Add the sound [s] to the following words:

admit	cough	hate	laugh	protect	smoke
appoint	crack	help	limit	remark	support

EXERCISE 141 Review the -*s* inflection. Add the sound [z] to the following words:

arrive	concern	disturb	flood	intend	open
blame	declare	divide	flow	join	perform
complain	deliver	drown	form	kill	prefer

EXERCISE 142 Review the tooth-ridge sounds. Pronounce the following words. Put your tongue tip on your tooth ridge for [l] and [n] and [d] and [t]. Turn your tongue tip upward for [r].

light	night	–	tight	right
lock	knock	dock	tock	rock
loom	–	doom	tomb	room
lose	–	dues	two's	ruse
lot	knot	dot	tot	rot
low	know	dough	toe	row
collect	connect	–	–	correct
dill	din	did	–	dear
file	fine	–	fight	fire
fill	fin	–	fit	fear
hill	–	hid	hit	hear
ill	in	id	it	ear
owl	–	–	out	our
till	tin	–	–	tear

EXERCISE 143 Practice the following, applying the principles previously discussed.

1. You'd better lock your door when you go out.
2. My car's developed a knock.
3. Have you paid your dues yet?
4. Your tot's growing very fast, isn't he?
5. Straighten the knot in your tie.
6. The janitor collects the garbage in the morning.
7. That fish has a long tail fin.
8. I've got a corn on my little toe.
9. The guests came in two's and three's.
10. You'll learn about the id in psychology.
11. She's a very dear friend of mine.
12. Bolivia produces a lot of tin.
13. She tried a ruse to get what she wanted.
14. Be sure to dot your *i*'s.
15. They're unloading at the dock now.
16. She's looking for that letter in the file.
17. Romeo and Juliet died in a tomb.
18. Everything I tell you goes in one ear and out the other.
19. She had tears in her eyes.
20. Owls fly at night, don't they?

76. 1— Do you ever listen to the radio?
    2— Yes, I do.
    1— What's your favorite program?
    2— Any news broadcast.

77. 1— English words are the hardest in the world.
    2— Why do you say that?
    1— I can't pronounce them.
    2— Whose fault is that?
    1— My parents'.

78. 1— Have you got used to drinking coffee?
    2— Not the kind Americans like.
    1— It's not bad.
    2— I suppose you can get used to anything.

79. 1— What do you have for breakfast?
    2— Toast and coffee.
    1— That's not enough.
    2— Oh, I have other things — like eggs and juice.

80. 1— Do you ever go to the theater?
    2— Every now and then.
    1— What kind of shows do you like?
    2— Musical comedies.

REVIEW: QUOTATIONS 45-46

45. "The time has come," the walrus said,
        "To talk of many things:
    Of shoes and ships and sealing wax —
        Of cabbages and kings — "
                                    — *Carroll*

46. Twinkle, twinkle, little star!
    How I wonder what you are,
    Up above the world so high,
    Like a diamond in the sky!
                                    — *Taylor*

LESSON 50 Two-Syllable Words: Stress on Second Syllable

The following words have stress on the second syllable. When you pronounce them, be sure to lengthen the stressed syllable.

1. [i] disease, extreme, increase (v), indeed, machine, receipt
2. [ɪ] insist, omit, permit (v), resist
3. [e] complaint, escape, exchange, explain, mistake
4. [ɛ] extent, forget, himself, hotel, immense, instead, intend, invent, myself, neglect, object (v), offend, offense, possess
5. [æ] command, demand
6. [ə] disgust, enough
7. [ɑ] garage, regard
8. [ɔ] applause, because, belong
9. [o] enclose, explode, oppose
11. [u] include, produce (v), reduce
12. [ɚ] observe, prefer, preserve
13. [aɪ] divide, entire, excite, inquire, invite, July, polite, provide
14. [aʊ] around, pronounce, surround
15. [ɔɪ] employ

EXERCISE 144 Practice the following, applying the principles previously discussed.

1. Flu is a contagious disease, isn't it?
2. Can you explain how you made that mistake?
3. A soldier has to obey a command.
4. You'd better put the car in the garage.
5. I've got to reduce.
6. Divide it equally.
7. Does that company employ students during the summer?
8. She couldn't resist buying that hat.
9. I wish I could invent something that would make a million dollars.
10. He gave up in disgust, didn't he?
11. Do these books belong to you?
12. She'll oppose everything he suggests.
13. Which do you prefer?
14. Pronounce it carefully.
15. He inquired where she lived.
16. They demanded their money back.

96

LESSON 51 *Going to* and *Used to*

Treat the combination *going to* indicating future time like an auxiliary: pronounce it [gɔɪŋtə]. Treat in the same way the combination *used to* indicating a habit in the past or having the meaning of "accustomed to": pronounce it [justə]. (*Use to* after *did* has the same pronunciation.) If either combination comes at the end of a sentence, stress the first vowel, and use [ʊ] for the last vowel: ['gɔɪŋtʊ] and ['justʊ].

EXERCISE 145 Practice the following, applying the principles previously discussed.

1. I used to like that boy, but now I don't.
2. It's going to rain, isn't it?
3. He said he was going to do it.
4. Have you got used to your new job?
5. Maria used to talk a lot in class.
6. What were you going to say?
7. She's going to call me tomorrow.
8. You aren't studying as hard as you said you were going to.
9. You used to say nice things to me.
10. Who's going to be the first speaker?
11. Is he ever going to stop talking?
12. Didn't you use to smoke?
13. David did whatever he said he was going to, didn't he?
14. You didn't use to speak to me like that.
15. My grandmother never got used to cars.
16. I'm going to leave.
17. He speaks better than he used to.
18. People are satisfied with what they're used to.
19. I haven't seen that movie, but I'm going to.
20. Do it the way you used to.
21. Did you use to think English was easy?
22. I've become used to teaching.

23. When are you going to go back to your country?
24. I used to see him every day.
25. He's going to give a speech tomorrow.
26. Riding used to make me have headaches.
27. John's going to go to Cuba tomorrow.
28. Food used to cost much less than it does now.
29. I'm going to stop now.
30. I'm not going to tell you.

EXERCISE 146 Review [ɛ] and [æ] and [ə]. Pronounce the following words, remembering that [ɛ] is lax; [æ] is tense, and [ə] is lax.

bed – bad – bud	hem – ham – hum
better – batter – butter	net – gnat – nut
dense – dance – dunce	pedal – paddle – puddle
fend – fanned – fund	pet – pat – putt
flesh – flash – flush	send – sand – sunned
guessed – gassed – gust	trek – track – truck

EXERCISE 147 Practice the following, applying the principles previously discussed.

1. Do you make your bed when you get up?
2. A dunce is a stupid person.
3. She fanned herself with a piece of paper.
4. Even if you can't sing, you can hum.
5. She put on a net after she washed her hair.
6. He's the teacher's pet, isn't he?
7. She got hit by a truck.
8. You need a stick of butter for your cake batter, don't you?
9. That was a bright flash of lightning.
10. His hat was blown off by a gust of wind.
11. Step on the brake pedal.
12. She sunned the clothes after she washed them.
13. He was gassed in the war.

LESSON 52   Difference in Voice

There are several pairs of related words which differ in pronunciation by the voicing or voicelessness of the last sound. All of those words which have a voiced final sound are verbs. Those which have a voiceless final sound are usually nouns. Sometimes the members of a pair differ in spelling; sometimes they do not.

Make the vowel before the voiced final consonant longer than the vowel before the voiceless final consonant.

EXERCISE 148   Pronounce the following pairs of words. The final sound of words in the first column is voiced. The final sound of words in the second column is voiceless.

abuse	abuse	intend	intent
advise	advice	misuse	misuse
believe	belief	mouth	mouth
close	close	prove	proof
descend	descent	relieve	relief
devise	device	save	safe
excuse	excuse	serve	serf
extend	extent	use	use
house	house		

EXERCISE 149   Five pairs of words differ not only in the last sound but also in the vowel sound. Pronounce the following pairs. The final sound of words in the first column is voiced. The final sound of words in the second column is voiceless.

bathe	bath
breathe	breath
choose	choice
clothe	cloth
lose	loss

EXERCISE 150   Practice the following, applying the principles previously discussed.

1. Don't abuse your books.
2. He has a right to his belief.
3. Will you excuse me, please?
4. The government will house the workers.
5. The dictator misused his power.

6. Do you have any proof?
7. That tablet will relieve my headache, won't it?
8. What's the use of worrying?
9. You breathe when you let your breath come in and out.
10. You'd better take my advice.
11. The descent was fast, wasn't it?
12. What was the extent of the damage?
13. I didn't intend to do that.
14. Say the sentences distinctly; don't mouth them.
15. Are you trying to save any money?
16. A serf had to serve his master.
17. You bathe in a bath tub.
18. Go ahead and choose: you have your choice.
19. Losing something is a loss.
20. She was clothed in black cloth.

REVIEW: DIALOGS 81-85

81. 1 — I'm going to write a book.
    2 — What about?
    1 — All the things a foreigner has to learn.
    2 — It'll be a best-seller.

82. 1 — If you had a lot of money, what would you buy?
    2 — An airplane.
    1 — What would you do with it?
    2 — I'd fly home this weekend.

83. 1 — Where's the post office?
    2 — I don't know.
    1 — It's around here somewhere.
    2 — Why don't you ask a policeman?

84. 1 — There's something that's bothering me.
    2 — What is it?
    1 — Do trees breathe?
    2 — Oh, yes, they certainly do.

85. 1 — What're you going to do on Sunday?
    2 — Study my lessons.
    1 — Aren't you going to church?
    2 — Probably.

47. Some ladies now make pretty songs,
    And some make pretty nurses.
Some men are good for righting wrongs,
    And some for writing verses.

                  — Locker-Lampson

48. All the world's a stage,
    And all the men and women merely players:
They have their exits and their entrances;
And one man in his time plays many parts,
His acts being seven ages.

                   — Shakespeare

49. Tiger! Tiger! burning bright
In the forests of the night,
What immortal hand or eye
Could frame thy fearful symmetry?

                   — Blake

LESSON 53   Words Ending in -age

A number of English words have an unstressed final syllable which contains the letters *-age*. The *-age* is pronounced [ɪdʒ]. Here are some examples of two-syllable words; the stress is on the first syllable:

average	courage	luggage	package	savage	village
baggage	damage	manage	passage	storage	voyage
breakage	language	message	postage	usage	wreckage

The words *carriage* and *marriage* are also two-syllable words with the stress on the first syllable; the final *-iage* is pronounced [ɪdʒ]. The word *mileage* is similar: [ˈmaɪlɪdʒ].

The following three-syllable words have the stress on the first syllable:

        orphanage   pilgrimage

The following three-syllable words have the stress on the second syllable:

      advantage   encourage   percentage

EXERCISE 151 Practice the following, applying the principles previously discussed.

1. It takes a lot of courage to do that.
2. What's your native language?
3. You'd better put your winter coat into storage, hadn't you?
4. Were there any messages while I was out?
5. What was the extent of the damage?
6. What's the mileage on the speedometer?
7. He got encouraging news from the doctor yesterday.
8. She grew up in an orphanage.
9. The people in the village were savage.
10. How much postage did you have to pay to send that package?
11. You won't be able to take much luggage on your voyage, will you?
12. You have to pay a breakage fee when you take a chemistry course.
13. They got a divorce after two years of marriage.
14. What're the advantages of living in the country?
15. No average man could manage on that salary, could he?

EXERCISE 152 Review group stress. Stress the noun: lengthen the stressed vowel. Don't stop between the words of the group.

for dessert	like a melody	a piece
the spirit	her statue	in front
of the library	the name	of a song
the truth	about English	the Romans
your teacher	a friend	your exams

LESSON 54 Two-Syllable Words: Stress on First Syllable

The following words have stress on the first syllable. When you pronounce them, be sure to lengthen the stressed vowel.

1. [i]   equal, even, evening, evil
2. [ɪ]   distance, distant, district, English, figure, finger, finish, guilty
3. [e]   daily, failure, faithful, famous, favor
4. [ɛ]   engine, enter, entrance, envy, essence, ever, every, extra, feather, fellow

5. [æ] badness, baggage, balance, barrel, basket, battle, cancel
6. [ə] dozen, funny, govern, humble, hundred, hunger
7. [ɑ] common, conquer, conquest, conscience, conscious, copper,
        contract (n)
8. [ɔ] awkward, border, broadcast, caution
9. [o] moment, mostly, motion
10. [ʊ] goodness
11. [u] future, human
12. [ɘ] earnest, firmly, furnish
13. [aɪ] heighten, idle, iron
14. [aʊ] coward, doubtful

EXERCISE 153 Practice the following, applying the principles previously discussed.

1. He left early last evening.
2. Do me a favor, please.
3. He's a nice fellow, isn't he?
4. I want a dozen eggs, please.
5. There was an awkward silence when he asked for suggestions.
6. What's the future of the human race?
7. I'm not a coward; I believe in using caution.
8. The plane covered a great distance in a few hours.
9. I've got to find out my bank balance.
10. She bought a set of copper frying pans.
11. I'll be with you in a moment.
12. Goodness is a virtue.
13. He firmly refused to tell me my score.
14. Workers are idle during a strike.
15. Her baggage was barrels and baskets.

EXERCISE 154 Review the past form. Add the sound [ɪd] to the following simple forms:

accept	concede	demand	neglect	resist
adopt	conclude	expect	operate	scold
arrest	collect	fade	predict	surround
appreciate	connect	include	present	translate
assist	correct	inherit	prevent	twist
attend	decide	invent	recommend	vote
avoid	defend	land	record	wade

EXERCISE 155 Review the past form. Add the sound [t] to the following simple forms:

announce	discuss	lack	promise	risk
attack	drop	like	provoke	rush
block	establish	possess	purchase	sacrifice
check	finish	preach	push	stop
confess	guess	produce	repress	switch

EXERCISE 156 Review the past form. Add the sound [d] to the following simple forms:

admire	borrow	describe	measure	repair
advise	claim	drag	observe	rescue
allow	climb	earn	oppose	seem
answer	consider	enjoy	praise	serve
arrange	control	explain	prefer	supervise
assign	cover	follow	prepare	threaten
believe	criticize	love	prove	train
belong	cure	marry	refuse	wonder

EXERCISE 157 Review [s] and [θ]. For [s], put your tongue tip near your upper front teeth, but don't touch them. For [θ], put your tongue tip lightly between your teeth. Don't stop your breath for either sound. Make both of them with much force.

sank – thank	some – thumb	bass – bath
saw – thaw	sought – thought	lass – lath
seem – theme	sud – thud	mass – math
sick – thick	sunder – thunder	miss – myth
sigh – thigh	useful – youthful	pass – path
sin – thin		truce – truth
sing – thing		use (noun) – youth
sink – think		worse – worth

EXERCISE 158 Practice the following, applying the principles previously discussed.

1. Did he thank you?
2. What's the theme of that song?
3. Don't sigh when I ask you a question.
4. Sing something sentimental.
5. I think that's right.

6. I thought you weren't going.
7. I can see a lath in that hole in the wall.
8. Did you pass the course?
9. That reference book is very useful, isn't it?
10. My headache is getting worse.
11. The ice will begin to thaw in March.
12. He wears thick glasses, doesn't he?
13. Is it always a sin to tell a lie?
14. That soap makes a lot of suds.
15. My thumb's sore.
16. That fish is a bass.
17. When's your math class?
18. A myth is a traditional story.
19. It's the truth.
20. My father acts very youthful.
21. Whatever is worth doing is worth doing well.

EXERCISE 159 Review [z] and [ð]. For [z], put your tongue tip near your upper front teeth, but don't touch them. For [ð], put your tongue tip lightly between your teeth. Don't stop your breath for either sound. Make both of them with little force.

z — thee	closing — clothing	breeze — breathe
	seizing — seething	close — clothe
		lays — lathe
		seize — seethe
		tease — teethe

EXERCISE 160 Practice the following, applying the principles previously discussed.

1. We don't use *thee* in conversation any more.
2. The breeze moved the leaves.
3. He saw a lathe in the machine shop.
4. I think he was trying to tease me.
5. Did you bring some warm clothing?
6. He was seething with anger.
7. When does that store close?
8. He told me to seize the opportunity.
9. How do we pronounce *z?*

EXERCISE 161 Review homophones. Pronounce the following pairs alike.

air – heir	groan – grown	road – rode
beat – beet	heard – herd	serf – surf
cellar – seller	loan – lone	steal – steel
doe – dough	pail – pale	wade – weighed

EXERCISE 162 Practice the following, applying the principles previously discussed.

1. The air in this room is bad.
2. Have you stopped beating your wife?
3. The child filled his pail with sand.
4. A female deer is a doe.
5. He's the heir to a large fortune.
6. When you bake dough, you get bread.
7. The child was pale after his sickness.
8. He heard a groan in the cellar.
9. I'm going to get a loan from the bank.
10. Do you like to wade in the surf?
11. He tried to steal a cow from the herd.
12. She poured vinegar over the beets.
13. *Dough* is a slang word for "money."
14. Sellers have to have buyers.

EXERCISE 163 Review the -s inflection. Add the sound [ɪz] to the following words:

address	cross	manage	pronounce	sacrifice
advise	discuss	memorize	propose	supervise
announce	establish	mix	publish	switch
arrange	fix	oppose	recognize	wash
astonish	introduce	please	reduce	watch
confess	judge	polish	rejoice	wish

EXERCISE 164 Review the -s inflection. Add the sound [s] to the following words:

accept	cultivate	invite	request	select
attack	defeat	lock	resent	stamp
attempt	develop	melt	resist	stop
attract	drop	omit	respect	suspect
check	expect	provoke	revoke	treat
conceal	imitate	repeat	risk	wipe

EXERCISE 165 Review the -s inflection. Add the sound [z] to the following words:

approve	contain	evade	preserve	retire
assign	control	examine	pretend	reveal
assume	defend	gather	prove	review
avoid	demand	guard	rain	sign
boil	descend	listen	receive	solve
breathe	describe	measure	recommend	supply
compare	employ	observe	renew	travel
conquer	end	prepare	reserve	try

REVIEW: DIALOGS 86-90

86. 1 – Do you like women's hats?
    2 – No, I don't.
    1 – Why not?
    2 – They don't look like hats.

87. 1 – Aren't you glad this week's over?
    2 – I certainly am.
    1 – What're you going to do this weekend?
    2 – Just rest.

88. 1 – I'm worried.
    2 – What's wrong?
    1 – I think I've lost my watch.
    2 – Oh, you probably left it at home.

89. 1 – Students have to buy a lot of things.
    2 – That's right – books and notebooks.
    1 – And pencils and pens.
    2 – It all adds up to a lot of money.

90. 1 – When's the next test?
    2 – We're going to have one today.
    1 – What's it on?
    2 – Words, probably.

50. Little Bo-Peep has lost her sheep
    And can't tell where to find them.
    Leave them alone and they'll come home
    And bring their tails behind them.

    — Anonymous

51. Laugh, and the world laughs with you;
    Weep, and you weep alone;
    For the sad old earth must borrow its mirth
    But has trouble enough of its own.

    — Wilcox

52. A flea and a fly in a flue
    Were imprisoned, so what could they do?
    Said the fly, "Let's flee."
    Said the flea, "Let's fly."
    So they flew through a flaw in the flue.

    — Anonymous

LESSON 55 Words Ending in -ous

A large number of words end in the letters *ous*. That ending is never stressed. It is pronounced [əs].

Words with -*ous* are very regular in location of stress. You can tell where the primary stress is from the spelling. Count the "vowel signs" before the -*ous*. A vowel sign is either a single vowel *letter* or a combination of vowel letters. The vowel letters are *a, e, i, o, u,* and *y* (except *u* after *q*, and *y* before a vowel).

Here are the rules:

1. If the word has only one vowel sign before the -*ous*, the stress is on that vowel sign. In the following examples, the stressed vowel sign is underlined.

f<u>a</u>mous	p<u>o</u>mpous	j<u>ea</u>lous
n<u>e</u>rvous	j<u>o</u>yous	gr<u>ie</u>vous

108

2. If the word has more than one vowel sign before the *-ous*, the stress is on the next to the last vowel sign. In the following examples the stressed vowel sign is underlined.

curious	continuous	dangerous	monotonous
envious	spontaneous	humorous	ridiculous
glorious	industrious	marvelous	mountainous
serious	mysterious	vigorous	treacherous
various	victorious	adventurous	villainous

There are no exceptions to the first rule. Rule 2 has relatively few exceptions, and all of those are stressed on the vowel sign before the *-ous*. Four rather common exceptions are "desirous," "disastrous," "enormous," and "tremendous."

The addition of the -ly ending for adverbs does not change the location of stress.

EXERCISE 166 Practice the following, applying the principles previously discussed.

1. I'm curious about what's going to happen next.
2. The northern part of Italy is very mountainous.
3. They're having a religious ceremony this morning.
4. Don't be suspicious; he's all right.
5. That was an obvious statement.
6. Certain kinds of mushrooms are poisonous.
7. He said that life in the army was monotonous.
8. Do you feel nervous before an exam?
9. He's a very famous author.
10. *Anon.* is an abbreviation for *anonymous*.
11. Where were you working previously?
12. Are you as studious as you ought to be?
13. He's very generous toward his children.
14. There's numerous things I've got to tell you.

EXERCISE 167 Review the past form. Add the sound [ɪd] to the following simple forms:

calculate	doubt	mend	regret	wait
comfort	guide	neglect	suggest	waste
disappoint	hesitate	record	surround	yield

EXERCISE 168 Review the past form. Add the sound [t] to the following simple forms:

crash	distinguish	miss	pronounce	sacrifice
crush	hope	mix	reach	watch

EXERCISE 169 Review the past form. Add the sound [d] to the following simple forms:

advertise	delay	offer	stay
arm	describe	order	study
care	determine	recognize	wander
carry	entertain	refer	welcome
compose	improve	rob	wonder
confuse	interfere	rub	yell

EXERCISE 170 Review [l] and [r]. Put your tongue tip on your tooth ridge for [l]. Turn your tongue tip upward for [r].

lace – race	lug – rug	glamor – grammar
law – raw	lute – route	glue – grew
led – red	blue – brew	plies – prize
limb – rim	cloud – crowd	elect – erect
list – wrist	flank – frank	hill – here
loom – room		till – tear

EXERCISE 171 Practice the following, applying the principles previously discussed.

1. They're going to erect a skyscraper there, aren't they?
2. The prize was an English grammar.
3. What else is on your list?
4. He broke his wrist when he slipped on the rug.
5. Her lips were red, and a tear glistened in her eye.
6. To be frank, I don't like crowds.
7. Unsolved problems always loom large in a person's mind, don't they?
8. The fastest runner will win the race.
9. Her wedding dress was made of lace.
10. They stayed till morning.
11. The clouds grew blacker in the blue sky.
12. She led the students out of the room.
13. We're going to elect a president soon.

110

14. Do you know how to play the lute?
15. I don't want to lug this heavy bag up that hill.
16. He took the shortest route to his home.
17. Do all girls want to have glamor?
18. It seems to be brewing up a storm.

EXERCISE 172 Review group stress. Stress the noun: lengthen the stressed vowel. Do not stop between the words of a group.

at my ease	a spear	the grave
its goal	to the seas	the sky
a star	in my days	of childhood
the ship	the prize	the port
the bells	the people	the night
with music	the cares	the day
their tents	like the Arabs	your hair

EXERCISE 173 Review initial [s] before consonants. Pronounce the following words. Make the [s] voiceless.

school	slice	sneer	speed	star
scream	slide	sneeze	spend	start
screen	smile	sniff	spent	sweep
skill	Smith	snore	spell	sweet
sleeve	smoke	snow	stand	swell
slender	smooth	speech	standard	swift

EXERCISE 174 Practice the following, applying the principles previously discussed.

1. He's at school.
2. Window screens keep out insects.
3. Roll up your sleeves.
4. Do you want sliced bread?
5. He smiled at her mistake.
6. A baby's skin is smooth.
7. Mr. Smith doesn't smoke.
8. Wake me up if I snore.
9. He's going to make a speech tomorrow.

10. Don't spend more than you earn.
11. How do you spell that?
12. Do you want the standard kind or the special?
13. She's got to sweep the floor.
14. Did your jaw swell when you had that tooth ache?
15. Did you hear a scream?
16. Practice develops your skill.
17. That floor is slippery: be careful, or you'll slide.
18. She wishes she were slender.
19. Don't sneer at his efforts.
20. Sneeze into your handkerchief.
21. She's never seen it snow before.
22. What's the speed of light?
23. He spent the night in a hotel.
24. She can't stand the sight of blood.
25. The stars were bright last night.
26. When do we start?
27. Her perfume smells too sweet.
28. Time passes very swiftly when you're busy.

LESSON 56 Three-Syllable Words: Stress on First Syllable

The following words have stress on the first syllable. When you pronounce them, be sure to lengthen the stressed vowel.

1. [i] recently, theater
2. [ɪ] interesting, liberty, minister, miserable, serious, sympathy, visitor
3. [e] neighborhood, radio
4. [ɛ] relative, remedy, restaurant, settlement, steadily, telegraph, telegram, telephone, temperature, tendency, terrible, various, yesterday
5. [æ] passenger, practical, rapidly, sacrifice, satisfy, Saturday, valuable
6. [ə] somebody, suddenly, wonderful
7. [ɑ] positively, possible, possibly, probable, probably, properly, property, quality, quantity

8. [ɔ] origin, ornament
9. [o] photograph, poetry
11. [u] universe, usual
12. [ə] permanent, personal, thoroughly
13. [aɪ] violence, violent

EXERCISE 175 Practice the following, applying the principles previously discussed.

1. Let's go to the theater tonight.
2. Turn down the radio.
3. I had a high temperature yesterday.
4. Somebody wonderful just went by.
5. Did you bring the ornaments for the Christmas tree?
6. They're carrying on business as usual.
7. I don't have any sympathy for students who don't study.
8. Does that satisfy your curiosity?
9. He's positively unbearable.
10. He took a photograph of the Statue of Liberty.
11. Do you have a permanent visa?
12. I've got a violent headache.

EXERCISE 176 Review homophones. Pronounce the following pairs alike.

aloud – allowed	hair – hare	rose – rows
berth – birth	hour – our	side – sighed
coarse – course	mail – male	suite – sweet
fair – fare	peace – piece	wait – weight

EXERCISE 177 Practice the following, applying the principles previously discussed.

1. Her mother has finally allowed her to have dates.
2. I hope it'll be fair tomorrow.
3. I'll meet you in an hour.
4. He wants peace at any price.
5. She sighed when I asked her a question.
6. They rented a suite in the hotel.

113

EXERCISE 177 (Continued)

7. What's your country of birth?
8. That thread is too coarse.
9. Australia's got a lot of hares.
10. Has the mail come yet?
11. The last two rows are empty.
12. What's your weight?

EXERCISE 178   Review [f] and [h] and [w] and [v] and [b].

```
fail – hail – wail – veil – bail
faced – haste – waste – vased – based
fair – hair – wear – vair – bear
file – heil – wile – vile – bile
fear – here – we're – veer – beer
fit – hit – wit – vit – bit
ferry – hairy – wary – very – berry
find – hind – wind – vined – bind
```

EXERCISE 179   Practice the following, applying the principles previously discussed.

1. Some of our best efforts are in vain.
2. His lawyer put up the bail to get him out of jail.
3. Be wary of women's wiles.
4. A vile odor came from the vent.
5. She feared to face her husband.
6. You'd better comb your hair and file your finger nails.
7. That baby wailed all night long.
8. His speech was based on his experience.
9. The wind suddenly veered to the west.
10. We're all very vain, you know.
11. Did you wind the clock?
12. Is it hailing now?
14. He shows a bit of wit in his verses, doesn't he?

EXERCISE 180   Review the past form. Add the sound [ɪd] to the following simple forms.

attend	direct	lift	provide	unite
avoid	float	load	separate	visit
depend	fold	profit	start	want

114

EXERCISE 181 Review the past form. Add the sound [t] to the following simple forms.

check	fish	look	produce	talk
cook	furnish	mark	punish	walk

EXERCISE 182 Review the past form. Add the sound [d] to the following simple forms.

apply	deceive	obey	smile
argue	enjoy	prove	tremble
bow	excuse	raise	turn
combine	handle	resign	worry
compare	hurry	return	woo
damage	mention	share	zoom

EXERCISE 183 Review [æ] and [ə] and [ɑ]. Pronounce the following words, remembering that [æ] is tense, [ə] is lax, and [ɑ] is tense.

babble – bubble – bobble   sadden – sudden – sodden
backs – bucks – box   shack – shuck – shock
cracks – crux – crocks   stack – stuck – stock

EXERCISE 184 Practice the following, applying the principles previously discussed.

1. Champagne has bubbles.
2. That's the crux of the problem.
3. You shuck corn before you cook it.
4. The baby babbled to himself contentedly.
5. The car got stuck in the mud.
6. He refers to his country home as a little shack.
7. She stored her butter in crocks.
8. Ask them to put it in a box.
9. The news saddened everybody.
10. I have a stack of papers waiting to be corrected.
11. You should fix the cracks before you paint, shouldn't you?
12. Don't take any stock in that rumor.
13. He showed his disappointment by saying, "Shucks!"

91. 1 — I've got a theory.
    2 — What is it?
    1 — There ought to be only one language in the world.
    2 — You'd have to learn it.
    1 — That's the catch.

92. 1 — What's that?
    2 — That's a lawn mower.
    1 — What's it for?
    2 — To cut grass.

93. 1 — Could I borrow some money from you?
    2 — How much do you want?
    1 — Five dollars.
    2 — All right.

94. 1 — I've made a great discovery.
    2 — What is it?
    1 — People are the same all over the world.
    2 — That's right.

95. 1 — Did you have a nice weekend?
    2 — Yes, I did.
    1 — What did you do?
    2 — A lot of things.

REVIEW: QUOTATIONS 53-55

53.   But the best I've known
    Stays here and changes, breaks, grows old, is blown
    About the winds of the world, and fades from brains
    Of living men, and dies.
                        Nothing remains.
                                    — *Brooke*

54. Yes, as the music changes,
        Like a prismatic glass,
    It takes the light and ranges
        Through all the moods that pass.
                                    — *Noyes*

55. For the moon never beams without bringing me dreams
    Of the beautiful Annabel Lee,
    And the stars never rise but I feel the bright eyes
    Of the beautiful Annabel Lee.

— Poe

LESSON 57 Wordings Ending in -ry

In words that end in -ry, the vowel letter before the -ry is silent in ordinary speech if the stress is on the syllable preceding that vowel letter. Examples are the following:

boundary ['baʊndrɪ]	misery ['mɪzrɪ]
delivery [dɪ'lɪvrɪ]	mystery ['mɪstrɪ]
every ['ɛvrɪ]	salary ['sælrɪ]
factory ['fæktrɪ]	satisfactory [sætɪs'fæktrɪ]
history ['hɪstrɪ]	slavery ['slevrɪ]
machinery [mə'ʃinrɪ]	victory ['vɪktrɪ]
memory ['mɛmrɪ]	

When some people speak slowly or emphatically, they pronounce a [ə] before the -ry; for example, *every* ['ɛvərɪ].

The vowel letter *a* or *e* before a final -ry is pronounced [ɛ] and has a secondary stress if the syllable before that vowel letter is not stressed. Some examples are the following:

cemetery ['sɛmətɛrɪ]	January ['dʒænjʊɛrɪ]
customary ['kəstəmɛrɪ]	necessary ['nɛsəsɛrɪ]
dictionary ['dɪkʃənɛrɪ]	secretary ['sɛkrətɛrɪ]
February ['fɛbrʊɛrɪ]	vocabulary [və'kæbjələrɪ]

EXERCISE 185 Practice the following, applying the principles previously discussed.

1. The farmers argued about their boundary line.
2. Every mystery ought to have a satisfactory explanation.
3. You would live in misery on my salary.
4. Is it necessary to go to the cemetery?

5. Is it customary to be nice to a secretary?
6. He's got a good memory, hasn't he?
7. I sent the letter by special delivery.
8. There's a lot of machinery in that factory, isn't there?
9. The victory brought an end to slavery.
10. February comes after January, doesn't it?
11. He bought a dictionary to increase his vocabulary.

EXERCISE 186 Review homophones. Pronounce the following pairs alike.

ail – ale	foul – fowl	rap – wrap
bare – bear	heal – heel	seam – seem
cell – sell	lessen – lesson	stair – stare
die – dye	packed – pact	vale – veil

EXERCISE 187 Practice the following, applying the principles previously discussed.

1. Do you like ale?
2. The prisoner was put in a cell.
3. The umpire called it a foul.
4. Has your wound healed yet?
5. The ministers signed the pact.
6. Girls worry about the seams of their stockings, don't they?
7. The room was bare.
8. She likes to dye her hair.
9. What ails that boy?
10. I hope your troubles will lessen.
11. Did you hear a rap?
12. You mustn't stare at people.
13. She's wearing a veil today.

EXERCISE 188 Review [s] and [z]. Pronounce the following pairs. Make [s] with much force; make [z] with little force.

bus – buzz	gross – grows	pace – pays
dense – dens	hiss – his	place – plays
dice – dies	juice – Jews	race – raise
dose – doze	lace – lays	since – sins
face – phase	lice – lies	spice – spies
fleece – flees	loss – laws	trace – trays
grace – graze	niece – knees	vice – vies

EXERCISE 189 Practice the following, applying the principles previously discussed.

1. Bees buzz.
2. That kind of flower dies in a week.
3. That's a phase of growing up.
4. Do you have a pair of fleece-lined gloves?
5. Borrow mine; don't take his.
6. That hen lays an egg almost every day.
7. He lies even when it would pay him to tell the truth.
8. It pays to be honest, doesn't it?
9. Most of the workers got a raise last month.
10. The woman vanished without a trace.
11. The lions rushed out of their dens.
12. He took a dose of medicine for his cough.
13. Does he say grace before eating?
14. He bought a gross of oranges.
15. There was a meeting between Catholics and Jews.
16. The plane was a total loss, wasn't it?
17. He left his money to his niece.
18. He's written a few plays.
19. I haven't seen him since yesterday.
20. Humor's the spice of life.
21. What's your worst vice?

LESSON 58   Three-Syllable Words: Stress on Second Syllable

The following words have stress on the second syllable. When you pronounce them, be sure to lengthen the stressed vowel.

1. [i]   idea, ideal
2. [ɪ]   official, omission, opinion, permission, position, religion, religious, resistance, suspicion, suspicious
3. [e]   quotation, relation
4. [ɛ]   perfection, possession, prevention, procession, profession, protection, reflection, remember, respectful, successful, suggestion, together, whatever, whenever, wherever

5. [æ] example, imagine, mechanic, tobacco
6. [ə] production, reduction, republic
7. [ɑ] forgotten, tomorrow
8. [ɔ] performance
9. [o] proposal
11. [u] inclusive, peculiar, solution
12. [ə] disturbance, encourage
13. [aɪ] horizon, inquiry, retirement
15. [ɔɪ] employment, enjoyment

EXERCISE 190 Practice the following, applying the principles previously discussed.

1. I've got an idea.
2. Did you memorize that quotation?
3. Children ought to be respectful.
4. The mechanic fixed the car.
5. That country's a republic.
6. There's no performance tonight.
7. He acts a little peculiar at times.
8. The sun came above the horizon.
9. He got a lot of enjoyment out of it.
10. What's your religion?
11. I'll do whatever you say.
12. Give me an example.
13. I can't imagine what you're doing.
14. Have you forgotten already?
15. What was their proposal?
16. Doesn't he ever encourage anybody?
17. Congress is making another inquiry.
18. There's been no official announcement.

LESSON 59 Words Ending in *-ic, -ics, -ical,* and *-ically*

Almost all words which end in *-ic, -ics, -ical,* or *-ically* have their primary stress on the vowel preceding those endings. Some examples are the following:

academic	economics	idiomatic	picnic
analytical	electrical	logically	poetic
artistically	energetic	mathematics	practical
Atlantic	enthusiastic	medical	public
automatically	epic	melodic	sarcastic
biographic	fanatic	methodical	Slavic
chemical	frantically	music	sympathetic
comic	garlic	optimistic	tropics
critical	gigantic	panic	typical
democratic	heroic	philosophical	whimsically
domestic	hysterical	photographic	zoologic

The major exceptions are these, with the stressed vowel underlined:

Arabic   Catholic   lunatic   rhetoric   politics

Arithmetic usually has primary stress on the first *i*. When it is used in phrases such as "arithmetic progression" and "arithmetic mean," it has primary stress on the *e*.

Adverbs which are related to words ending in -*ic* and -*ical* have the ending -*ically*. The only exception is *publicly*, and that has the stress on the *u*.

EXERCISE 191 Practice the following, applying the principles previously discussed.

1. Are you going on the picnic?
2. Don't be too critical about other people's domestic manners.
3. There was a tragic traffic accident at that corner.
4. You can't be romantic with a sarcastic girl, can you?
5. Can you be aristocratic and democratic at the same time?
6. Do you feel energetic early in the morning?
7. You'd better go to the Medical Office to see about your finger.
8. She puts a lot of garlic in her tomato sauce, doesn't she?
9. When people start talking philosophically, they frequently become pessimistic.

EXERCISE 191 (Continued)

10. In linguistics, you study grammatical patterns and syntactical relationships.
11. When he gets enthusiastic about something, he always sounds emphatic.
12. He's a very prosaic sort of fellow: he can't appreciate anything poetic.
13. He's taking physics and economics.

EXERCISE 192 Review initial [s] before consonants. Pronounce the following words. Make the [s] voiceless.

skin	slight	spin	state	swim
skirt	slim	spirit	station	swing
sky	slip	spite	stay	Swiss
square	slipper	splendid	steady	
	slope	split	steal	
	slow	spoil	steam	
		sport	steel	
		spot	steer	
		spread	stop	
		spring	stick	

EXERCISE 193 Practice the following, applying the principles previously discussed.

1. Do you like square dancing?
2. That's the spirit! Don't give up.
3. He's got a new Swiss watch.
4. Do you want to go swimming?
5. Don't spoil their fun.
6. Where are my slippers?
7. In spite of all my efforts, I still make mistakes.
8. The sky's pretty in the spring.
9. He's slow but sure.
10. He was a slim young man.
11. How long did you stay there?
12. Her skirt has spots on it.
13. Get off at the next station.
14. That's a nice-looking sport shirt.
15. You ought to stop spreading that rumor.
16. Why don't you stay?
17. He splits his profits with his partner.

EXERCISE 194 Review homophones. Pronounce the following pairs alike.

ate – eight	hail – hale	sail – sale
blew – blue	knew – new	soar – sore
colonel – kernel	meat – meet	tacked – tact
fir – fur	plain – plane	way – weigh

EXERCISE 195 Practice the following, applying the principles previously discussed.

1. The plane leaves at eight o'clock.
2. He's a colonel in the army.
3. Hail is frozen rain, isn't it?
4. He doesn't eat meat on Friday.
5. Gulls soar above the ocean.
6. Use tact when you ask him that.
7. The referee blew his whistle.
8. She bought a fir tree for Christmas.
9. I knew him in Chicago.
10. The children are sailing their boats in the pond.
11. Which way did they go?

REVIEW: DIALOGS 96-100

96. 1 – Have you studied very much this semester?
     2 – An awful lot.
     1 – As much as you could?
     2 – Well, maybe not.

97. 1 – Christmas is coming.
         I certainly am glad.
     2 – I have to go shopping.
     1 – Do you know what you're going to buy?
     2 – Not yet.

98. 1 – Did you come to school yesterday?
     2 – No, I didn't.
     1 – Why didn't you?
     2 – I didn't feel well.

REVIEW: DIALOGS (Continued)

99. 1 — Where can I get some razor blades?
    2 — At the drugstore.
    1 — Do you want to go with me?
    2 — All right.

100. 1 — Do you know any "tongue twisters"?
    2 — What are they?
    1 — Things like "Peter Piper picked a peck of pickled
          peppers."
    2 — Oh, yes, we have them in my language.

REVIEW: QUOTATIONS 56-58

56. And here's the happy, bounding flea —
You can not tell the he from she.
The sexes look alike, you see;
But she can tell, and so can he.

                    — Young

57. Out of the night that covers me,
    Black as the Pit from pole to pole,
I thank whatever gods may be
    For my unconquerable soul.

                    — Henley

58. A tutor who tooted the flute
Tried to teach two young tooters to toot.
    Said the two to the tutor,
    "Is it harder to toot or
To tutor two tooters to toot?"

                    — Wells

LESSON 60 Two-Syllable Words: Stress on First Syllable

The following words have stress on the first syllable. When you pronounce them, be sure to lengthen the stressed vowel.

1. [i]   season, secret, speaker
2. [ɪ]   spirit, strictly, system, ticket, victory, village, visit, whisper

3. [e] payment, player, sacred, safety, sailor

4. [ɛ] several, shelter, special, splendid, steady, temper, temple, tender, therefore, threaten, treasure

5. [æ] narrow, natural, package, parent, passage, practice, rapid, rather

6. [ə] substance, sudden, suffer, summer, Sunday, supper, thunder

7. [ɑ] pocket, polish, positive, problem, product, profit, progress (n)

8. [ɔ] often, order, organ

9. [o] program, shoulder, slowly

10. [ʊ] woman

11. [u] student, truly

12. [ɚ] Thursday, virtue, worker

13. [aɪ] silence, silent, slightly

14. [aʊ] powder

EXERCISE 196 Practice the following, applying the principles previously discussed.

1. I know a secret.
2. The boiler has a safety valve.
3. Do you remember that passage in the book?
4. The bookstore will order the book for you.
5. She's a very nice woman, isn't she?
6. Are you coming to class on Thursday?
7. I feel slightly tired.
8. Do you have a ticket to the show?
9. Don't lose your temper; be calm.
10. It often thunders in the summer.
11. He's making good progress in English.
12. My coat doesn't fit across the shoulders.
13. I'm truly sorry.
14. She's going to powder her nose.
15. That's the spirit; don't give up.

LESSON 61 Words Ending in -ate

More than four hundred words of more than one syllable end in the letters -ate. Some are used as verbs; some are used as adjectives; some are used as nouns; and some are used as two parts of speech. Both the pronunciation of the -ate and the place of stress in the word depend upon the part of speech the word is used as. The few exceptions are discussed separately below.

The ending -ate is pronounced [et] if the word is used as a verb. It is pronounced [ɪt] if the word is used as an adjective or as a noun.

The [ɪt] is never stressed. In two-syllable words, the stress is on the syllable preceding the [ɪt]; for example, climate, pirate, private, and senate. In words with more than two syllables, the stress is on the second syllable before the [ɪt]. In the examples below, the stressed vowel is underlined.

The [et] usually has primary stress in words of two syllables; for example, create, debate, dictate, locate, relate, and translate. In words with more than two syllables, the [et] has a secondary stress, and the primary stress is on the second syllable before the [et].

Most of the exceptions to the above rules are nouns in which the -ate is pronounced [et]. Only one of those, debate, has primary stress on the -ate. All the other two-syllable nouns have the primary stress on the preceding syllable — inmate, nitrate, phosphate, playmate, roommate, and schoolmate. Two three-syllable nouns have the primary stress on the first syllable: concentrate and potentate. Two adjectives, innate and sedate, are also exceptions: they have stressed [et].

EXERCISE 197 Pronounce the following adjectives and nouns. Stress the underlined vowel. Pronounce the final -ate as [ɪt].

accurate	considerate	graduate	separate
adequate	consulate	immediate	subordinate
affectionate	delegate	intimate	syndicate
alternate	deliberate	legitimate	temperate
appropriate	delicate	moderate	ultimate
certificate	desperate	passionate	unfortunate
chocolate	fortunate	predicate	vertebrate

126

EXERCISE 198 Pronounce the following verbs. The underlined vowel has primary stress, and the final *-ate* is pronounced [et] with secondary stress.

accommodate	concentrate	educate	imitate
alternate	congratulate	elaborate	indicate
anticipate	contemplate	elevate	isolate
appreciate	cooperate	eliminate	nominate
appropriate	cultivate	estimate	operate
associate	decorate	exaggerate	originate
celebrate	delegate	graduate	regulate
circulate	demonstrate	hesitate	separate
communicate	dominate	illustrate	suffocate

EXERCISE 199 Practice the following, applying the principles previously discussed.

1. I want a chocolate soda.
2. Did you get a certificate when you finished the course?
3. The delegates nominated Mr. White.
4. You can have your mail sent to the consulate, can't you?
5. I want to congratulate you on your success.
6. Mr. Peters certainly dominates his wife.
7. He who hesitates is lost.
8. The doctor is going to operate on her for appendicitis.
9. He gave a very elaborate explanation.
10. How do you operate that machine?
11. You must be considerate of other people's feelings.
12. Don't hesitate; do it now.
13. Is your cat affectionate?
14. You're illiterate if you can't read.
15. What do you estimate it's worth?
16. You'll get along better with people if you cooperate with them.
17. I certainly appreciate your help.
18. We're going to decorate the Christmas tree.
19. Did he graduate from college?
20. Write on alternate lines.
21. If you rub your eye, you'll irritate it.
22. That dress isn't appropriate for the occasion.

23. Did the salesman demonstrate how to use it?
24. He says he's going to dedicate his book to his wife.
25. I've got to have my watch regulated.
26. Rumors circulate awfully fast, don't they?
27. Why was he eliminated from the race?
28. He doesn't like chocolate ice cream.
29. That woman certainly dominates her husband.

EXERCISE 200 Review [l] and [r]. Put your tongue tip on your tooth ridge for [l]. Turn your tongue tip upward for [r].

laughter — rafter	loyal — royal	glow — grow
leap — reap	lust — rust	pleasant — present
lice — rice	bloom — broom	collect — correct
light — write	climb — crime	fill — fear
long — wrong	flame — frame	owl — our
	fly — fry	

EXERCISE 201 Practice the following, applying the principles previously discussed.

1. There was a great deal of laughter after his announcement.
2. You'll need light clothes for the summer.
3. If you leave your bicycle out in the rain, it'll rust.
4. Look before you leap.
5. Do you put butter on rice?
6. I won't be gone long.
7. He's very loyal to all his friends.
8. Have you seen the flowers in bloom in the park?
9. We watched the man climb up the telephone pole.
10. You can grow some plants in water.
11. The weather's very pleasant today.
12. You have nothing to fear, do you?
13. An owl flies at night.
14. Put the pot over the flame.
15. He's going to fly to Europe next week, isn't he?
16. I need somebody to correct my spelling.
17. Put the broom in the closet.

LESSON 62 Two-Syllable Words: Stress on First Syllable

The following words have stress on the first syllable. When you pronounce them, be sure to lengthen the stressed vowel.

1. [i] teacher, treatment, weaken, weakness, weekly
2. [ɪ] whistle, wicked, widow, window, winter, wisdom, witness, women
3. [e] slavery, statement, station, straighten, stranger
4. [ɛ] tremble, very, vessel, wealthy, weapon, weather, Wednesday welcome, western, whether
5. [æ] saddle, sample, scatter, shadow, standard, travel, valley, value
6. [ə] trouble, uncle, under, upper, upward, wonder
7. [ɑ] promise, promptly, proper, solemn, solid, swallow, wander
8. [ɔ] quarter, royal, shortly, strongly
9. [o] social, soldier, total, wholly
10. [ʊ] wooden
11. [u] Tuesday, union, unit
12. [ɚ] workmen, worry, worship
13. [aɪ] title, trial, widely
14. [aʊ] power, tower

EXERCISE 202 Practice the following, applying the principles previously discussed.

1. He's undergoing treatment for his leg injury.
2. She was trembling from the cold.
3. The crowd scattered when somebody fired a gun.
4. A quarter of the time he does nothing at all.
5. Have you ever worn a pair of wooden shoes?
6. Don't worry; everything'll be all right.
7. I can't remember the title of that book.
8. Were there any witnesses at the trial?
9. He's going to the station to see his wife off.
10. I wonder what's troubling her.
11. He gave me his solemn promise that he would come next Wednesday.
12. You're wholly right.
13. All the employees are members of a union.
14. The planes receive directions from the control tower.
15. He whistled when he heard the news.
16. My uncle's arriving on Tuesday.

129

LESSON 63 Words Ending in -ture and -sure

Unstressed -*ture* at the end of a word is pronounced [tʃə]. Some examples are the following:

adventure	feature	furniture	lecture	mixture	picture
creature	fixture	future	literature	nature	temperature

The words *mature*, *immature*, and *premature* have stress on the -*ture*, which is pronounced [tʃʊr].

Unstressed -*sure* at the end of a word is pronounced [ʒə]. Some examples are *measure*, *pleasure*, and *treasure*.

The word *pressure* is pronounced ['prɛʃə].

The words *insure* and *assure* are stressed on the last syllable: [ɪn'ʃʊr] and [ə'ʃʊr].

EXERCISE 203 Practice the following, applying the principles previously discussed.

1. They're buying a lot of furniture for their new house.
2. Did you like the feature picture?
3. He promised to study harder in the future.
4. It was a pleasure to do it.
5. Don't let the salesman pressure you into buying something you don't want.
6. That's just human nature, isn't it?
7. What's the temperature now?
8. They're going to sell the fixtures before they tear down that building.
9. That boy certainly acts mature.
10. Do you hope to find a hidden treasure?
11. You'd better insure the package when you mail it.
12. I assure you I feel all right.

EXERCISE 204 Review [l] and [r]. Put your tongue tip on your tooth ridge for [l]. Turn your tongue tip upward for [r].

lap – rap	lot – rot	glass – grass
lays – raise	lure – Ruhr	play – pray
lest – rest	bleed – breed	plowed – proud
line – Rhine	clash – crash	dill – dear
load – road	clue – crew	little – litter
	flesh – fresh	

130

EXERCISE 205 Practice the following, applying the principles previously discussed.

1. She put her napkin in her lap.
2. Let's take a rest.
3. He loaded his gun.
4. Don't let television lure you away from your studies.
5. Do they have any clues about the crime?
6. He broke the glass in the mirror.
7. He's proud his son won the race.
8. Little children are likely to litter their room a lot.
9. Raise your hand if you want to speak.
10. They took a boat trip down the Rhine.
11. Do you read a lot?
12. Familiarity breeds contempt.
13. The vase fell to the floor with a crash.
14. Be sure to buy fresh flowers.
15. The school has a large playground.
16. Dear me! What am I going to do?
17. He plowed the field and planted the grass.

REVIEW: DIALOGS 101-105

101. 1 – Are you going anywhere this weekend?
    2 – No, I'm going to stay here.
    1 – There're a lot of ways of having fun in town.
    2 – Fun? I've got to study.

102. 1 – You're coming back next semester, aren't you?
    2 – Yes, I am.
    1 – What're you going to take?
    2 – A lot of courses.

103. 1 – I've lost a book.
    2 – Where'd you lose it?
    1 – In the library.
    2 – That's too bad.

104. 1 – Do you know the names of the days of the week?
    2 – Of course I do.
    1 – Do you always pronounce *Thursday* correctly?
    2 – I try to.

105. 1 – What do you want for dessert?
     2 – A piece of cherry pie.
     1 – Do you want some ice cream on it?
     2 – No, thank you.

REVIEW: QUOTATIONS 59-61

59. Immortality is not a gift;
    Immortality is an achievement;
    And only those who strive mightily
    Shall possess it.

– Masters

60. Bowed by the weight of centuries, he leans
    Upon his hoe and gazes on the ground,
    The emptiness of ages in his face,
    And on his back the burden of the world.

– Markham

61. There was an old man with a beard
    Who said, "It is just what I feared!
       Two owls and a hen,
       Four larks and a wren
    Have all built their nests in my beard."

– Lear

LESSON 64 Four-Syllable Words: Stress on Second Syllable

The following words have stress on the second syllable. When you pronounce them, be sure to lengthen the stressed vowel.

1. [i]   immediate, obedience, obedient
2. [ɪ]   ability, activity, additional, certificate, conditional, continuous, efficiency, experience, material, mysterious, original, particular, political, simplicity
3. [e]   available, occasional
4. [ɛ]   competitor, development, electrical, essentially, experiment, professional, successfully
5. [æ]   comparison, congratulate, grammatical, mechanical, reality
6. [ə]   industrial

7. [ɑ] apologize, apology, astonishing, astonishment, democracy, equality, impossible, responsible
12. [ə] encouragement
13. [aɪ] advisable, anxiety, society, variety
15. [ɔɪ] enjoyable

EXERCISE 206 Practice the following, applying the principles previously discussed.

1. I got an immediate reply to my letter.
2. Is Mr. Gibson available now?
3. A professional man has to worry about competitors just like a business man.
4. You were responsible for that, and you ought to apologize.
5. He wants some additional experience in political activity.
6. He bought his son a mechanical toy.
7. Are you interested in industrial unions?

LESSON 65 Words with x

The letter x represents different sounds in different words. However, you can usually tell how an x in a particular word is pronounced.

1. x is usually pronounced [ks].

ax	oxygen	taxi	explode
axis	excuse	wax	express
mix	exercise	expense	extract
expression	sex	experience	extend
box	tax	experiment	extra
exchange	expand	extraordinary	extreme
next	expect	explain	fix

In words spelled with *exce-* and *exci-*, there is only one [s]; for example, *except, excite, exceed, excellent,* and *excess.*

2. x at the beginning of a word is pronounced [z]. There are not many English words that begin with an x. Two examples are *Xavier* and *xylophone.*

3. x before a stressed vowel is pronounced [gz].

exact	exaggerate	examination	exist
exact¹y	examine	example	

The *h* in the words *exhaust, exhibit, exhilarate,* and *exhort* is not pronounced; the stress is on the vowels after the *h;* therefore, the *x* is pronounced [gz].

4. In a few words, x represents special pronunciations:

anxiety [æŋ'zaɪətɪ]   luxury ['ləkʃərɪ]

anxious ['æŋʃəs]   luxurious [ləg'ʒʊrɪəs]

x-ray ['ɛks're]

The *x* in *exile* and *exit* may be pronounced either as [ks] or as [gz]. The abbreviation *Xmas* is pronounced like the full form *Christmas.*

EXERCISE 207   Practice the following, applying the principles previously discussed.

1. The boy broke the box with an ax.
2. There's no excuse for not knowing that expression.
3. Don't exaggerate; tell me exactly what happened.
4. Taxis are expensive.
5. What do you expect he'll do next?
6. She has a luxurious apartment.
7. You'll need some oxygen for your experiment, won't you?
8. He excused her from the examination.
9. I'm exhausted.
10. He got extremely nervous about the exhibit.
11. I'm anxious to know what the x-ray will show.

EXERCISE 208   Review [l] and [r].   Put your tongue tip on your tooth ridge for [l].   Turn your tongue tip upward for [r].

late – rate	lung – rung	gland – grand
lay – ray	bled – bread	plate – prate
lent – rent	blush – brush	plow – prow
lime – rhyme	clown – crown	miller – mirror
liver – river	fleas – freeze	ill – ear
lose – ruse		towel – tower

EXERCISE 209 Practice the following, applying the principles previously discussed.

1. Did you have to pay a late fee?
2. They're going up on my rent again.
3. We took a cruise up the river Sunday.
4. Pneumonia's a disease of the lungs.
5. Do boys blush more often than girls?
6. I thought I'd freeze last night.
7. Put the sandwiches on a plate.
8. He says his ear aches.
9. Well, that's one ray of hope.
10. Limes are green or yellow.
11. Let's do it. What've we got to lose?
12. He bled quite a bit after the operation.
13. Don't act like a clown.
14. Where's your thyroid gland?
15. Look at yourself in the mirror.
16. Hand me a towel, please.

EXERCISE 210 Review difference in stress. Pronounce the nouns in the first column with stress on the first syllable. Pronounce the verbs in the second column with stress on the second syllable. Lengthen the stressed vowel.

escort	escort	refuse	refuse
import	import	subject	subject
project	project	survey	survey
protest	protest	suspect	suspect
rebel	rebel	transfer	transfer
record	record		

EXERCISE 211 Practice the following, applying the principles previously discussed.

1. What's your hardest subject?
2. The government's building that housing project.
3. She rebels against any sort of discipline, doesn't she?
4. The police are questioning a suspect.
5. How was your record in high school?

6. Did he refuse to listen to you?
7. He's in the import-export business.
8. Didn't you make a protest about your grade?
9. He's teaching a survey of English literature, isn't he?
10. Be sure to get a transfer when you get on the bus.
11. Were you subjected to mistreatment?

EXERCISE 212 Review [d] and [ð]. Put your tongue tip on your tooth ridge for [d]. Put your tongue lightly between your teeth for [ð]. Both sounds are voiced; make them gently.

dare – there	dough – though	load – loathe
den – then	breed – breathe	seed – seethe

EXERCISE 213 Review [t] and [θ]. Put your tongue tip on your tooth ridge for [t]. Put your tongue lightly between your teeth for [θ]. Both sounds are voiceless; make them strongly.

taught – thought	tread – thread	debt – death
tick – thick	true – through	fort – fourth
tin – thin	boat – both	pat – path
torn – thorn		

EXERCISE 214 Practice the following, applying the principles previously discussed.

1. What happened after you got there?
2. He married again after his wife's death.
3. It's strange but true.
4. Did you have to go in debt to buy it?
5. Don't forget to get a pat of butter with your bread.
6. His hair used to be thick, but now it's very thin.
7. I eat chocolates even though I shouldn't.
8. That's the fourth time I've told you that.
9. I'll talk with both of you in a minute.
10. That's harder than I thought it would be.
11. Flies breed in filth.
12. I wish your watch didn't tick so loud.

EXERCISE 215 Review [ə] and vowel and [r]. Pronounce the following groups. Turn your tongue tip upward for [ə] and [r].

lurk	–	–	lark	–	–
pert	–	–	part	port	–
shirt	–	–	–	short	–
spur	spear	spare	spar	spore	spoor
turn	–	–	–	torn	–
word	weird	–	–	ward	–
–	cheer	chair	char	chore	–
–	fierce	–	farce	force	–
–	mere	mayor	mar	more	Moore
–	rear	rare	–	roar	Ruhr
–	tear	tear	tar	tore	tour

EXERCISE 216 Practice the following, applying the principles previously discussed.

1. You haven't heard a word I've said.
2. Teen-age girls are frequently pert.
3. He was wearing a shirt and a pair of shorts.
4. The audience gave a cheer when he got up from his chair.
5. It's a farce when he tries to act fierce.
6. A strange man has been lurking around the house after dark.
7. She did it on the spur of the moment.
8. The laundry's torn my new shirt.
9. Mr. Moore is running for mayor.
10. You can hear the lions roar in the zoo.
11. Are you going on the tour today?

LESSON 66 Two-Syllable Words: Stress on First Syllable

The following words have stress on the first syllable. When you pronounce them, be sure to lengthen the stressed vowel.

1. [i] female, fever, freedom, frequent (adj)
2. [ɪ] hinder, history, illness, insect, instant, interest, inward, issue, kingdom
3. [e] favorite, flavor, graceful, grateful

4. [ɛ]   friendly, friendship, general, generous, gentle, gently, healthy, heaven, heavy, jealous, leather
5. [æ]   captain, carriage, carry, castle, cattle, damage, factory
6. [ə]   hungry, hunter, husband, judgment, justice, lovely, lucky
7. [ɑ]   copy, cottage, cotton, darkness, doctor, dollar, farmer
8. [ɔ]   cautious, coffee, corner
9. [o]   motor, noble, notebook
10. [ʊ]   plural
11. [u]   jewel, loosen
12. [ɚ]   further, hurry, journey
13. [ɑɪ]   item, island
14. [ɑʊ]   doubtless

EXERCISE 217   Practice the following, applying the principles previously discussed.

1. Don't you believe in freedom of speech?
2. That ballet dancer is very graceful.
3. He's the captain of the ship.
4. The doctor has a small cottage on the seashore.
5. What's the plural of *woman?*
6. I don't like to hurry to get ready to go on a journey.
7. He doubtless had a reason for saying that.
8. I hope nothing will hinder your progress.
9. Do you have a leather jacket?
10. Doesn't that smell make you hungry?
11. Be cautious when you turn the corner.
12. The motor needs oiling.
13. He loosened his belt after eating.
14. What would you take to read on a deserted island?

REVIEW: DIALOGS 106-110

106. 1 – Have you finished your exams?
      2 – No. Just half of them.
      1 – Will you take the rest next week?
      2 – No. This week.

107.
1– Have you heard the rumor about George Smith?
2– No. What is it?
1– He's lost his job.
2– That may be just gossip.
1– Yes. You can't believe everything you hear.

108.
1– Did you have a nice weekend?
2– Yes, I did. Did you?
1– A very pleasant one.
2– We ought to have another one right away.

109.
1– What're you going to take next semester?
2– Probably history, a science course, and some more English.
1– You're going to have to work hard.
2– Even harder than I did this semester.

110.
1– A pretty girl's like a melody.
2– That's the name of a song.
1– It's the truth, too.
2– I agree.

REVIEW: QUOTATIONS 62-63

62. The curfew tolls the knell of parting day,
The lowing herd winds slowly o'er the lea,
The plowman homeward plods his weary way
And leaves the world to darkness and to me.

— *Gray*

63. ... let us be true
To one another! for the world, which seems
To lie before us like a land of dreams
So various, so beautiful, so new,
Has really neither joy, nor love, nor light,
Nor certitude, nor peace, nor help for pain.

— *Arnold*

LESSON 67 Words with -ci-, -si-, and -ti-

Words which have any of the following endings are stressed on the vowel preceding the ending:

(-ci-)   -cial, -cian, -cience, -ciency, -cient, -cion, -cious

(-si-)   -sian, -sion

(-ti-)   -tial, -tian, -tience, -tient, -tion, -tional, -tious

With few exceptions, the -ci-, -sci-, -si-, -ssi-, and -ti- in those words are all pronounced [ʃ]. Don't pronounce the i's separately. Here are some examples:

EXERCISE 218   Practice the following, applying the principles previously discussed.

artificial	suspicion	conscious	description
commercial	precious	subconscious	direction
official	suspicious	unconscious	mention
social	Russian	dimension	motion
special	confession	extension	nation
musician	discussion	essential	additional
physician	expression	patience	national
politician	permission	patient	cautious
efficiency	possession	action	fictitious
ancient	profession	ambition	flirtatious
efficient	conscience	application	infectious

EXERCISE 219   The -ti- in the endings in Lesson 67 is pronounced [tʃ] if it is preceded by an s. Practice pronouncing the following words:

> Christian   question   suggestion

EXERCISE 220   The -si- in the endings in Lesson 67 is pronounced [ʒ] if it is preceded by a vowel, including [ə]. Practice pronouncing the following words:

decision	explosion	occasion	conversion
division	confusion	diversion	Persian

EXERCISE 221 Practice the following, applying the principles previously discussed.

1. Do you like artificial flowers?
2. Don't lose your patience with children.
3. Did you fill out an application for admission?
4. The musician played special songs for the occasion.
5. His conscience is bothering him.
6. There was no mention of their decision in the national papers.
7. The price of admission is seventy-five cents.
8. It's essential to practice, isn't it?
9. We're suspicious about his so-called confession.
10. A politician is usually cautious.
11. The physician wrote out a prescription for the patient.
12. The officials gave an extension to his petition.

EXERCISE 222 Review group stress. Stress the noun: lengthen the stressed vowel. Do not stop between the words of a group.

the winds	of the world	from his brain
the music	the light	the moon
out of the night	from the office	to the teacher
a gift	of centuries	the stars
upon his hand	the sexes	on the ground
the emptiness	with a friend	of ages

EXERCISE 223 Review [s] and [ʃ]. Put your tongue tip near your upper front teeth for [s]. Protrude your lips for [ʃ]. Do not stop your breath for either sound. Both sounds are voiceless. Make them with much force.

sack – shack	seek – sheik	sealed – shield
said – shed	seep – sheep	subtle – shuttle
sake – shake	self – shelf	sue – shoe
sale – shale	sin – shin	sun – shun
	sip – ship	

EXERCISE 224   Practice the following, applying the principles previously discussed.

1. He put the sack of potatoes in the shack.
2. You can sometimes find oil in shale.
3. A sheik is the leader of a group of Arabs.
4. Don't make a noise when you sip your coffee.
5. His former friends shun him these days.
6. That coat will shed rain, won't it?
7. I'll have a vanilla milk shake.
8. He sealed the letter with wax.
9. He told me that himself.
10. The boys are trying to shin up the pole.
11. You can take the shuttle train to the station.
12. I want to get a shoe shine.

EXERCISE 225   Review homophones. Pronounce the following pairs alike.

ball – bawl	hear – here	scene – seen
break – brake	know – no	some – sum
dear – deer	massed – mast	tail – tale
flea – flee	pole – poll	weak – week

EXERCISE 226   Practice the following, applying the principles previously discussed.

1. Cinderella went to the ball.
2. She's a dear little thing.
3. What do you hear from your family?
4. I don't know what to do.
5. They're taking an opinion poll.
6. Have you seen him lately?
7. Don't pull the cat's tail.
8. I've been here only a week.
9. Put the brakes on to hold the car.
10. In books, people flee from danger; in conversation, they run away from it.
11. People were massed in Times Square on New Year's Eve.
12. Sometimes it seems everything goes wrong, doesn't it?
13. That baby is bawling again.

LESSON 68 Two-Syllable Words: Stress on First Syllable

The following words have stress on the first syllable. When you pronounce them, be sure to lengthen the stressed vowel.

1. [i]   people, reader, reason, recent
2. [ɪ]   quickly, river, signal, silver, simple, simply, single, sister
3. [e]   neighbor, painter, paper, patience, patient
4. [ɛ]   pressure, question, ready, reference, rescue, second, sel-
            dom, sentence, separate (adj), settle
5. [æ]   manage, manner, marry, marriage, married, master, matter
6. [ə]   something, somewhere, stomach, struggle, study, subject (n)
7. [ɑ]   modern, modest, nonsense, object (n), pardon, partly, party
8. [ɔ]   loyal, morning, northern
9. [o]   owner, poem, poet
10. [ʊ]   surely
11. [u]   pupil, ruler
12. [ɚ]   service, surface, thorough
13. [aɪ]   quiet, rival, science
14. [aʊ]   output

EXERCISE 227 Practice the following, applying the principles previously discussed.

1. People say they're in love.
2. If you're a painter, you have to be patient.
3. I can hardly manage on my salary.
4. He won't put up with any nonsense in his class, will he?
5. The poet recited one of his own poems.
6. You'd better draw that line with a ruler.
7. They're rivals for the prize.
8. That factory's been increasing its output steadily.
9. A bachelor's a single man.
10. Do your children sleep in separate beds?
11. What's your favorite subject?
12. She comes from the northern part of the state.
13. Surely, you don't mean that, do you?
14. They made a thorough search of the office.
15. That paper is smooth.
16. The submarine came to the surface.
17. He's a modest author.

LESSON 69 Words with [j]

The sound [j] is frequently represented by the letters *y* or *i* before a vowel, as in *you, year, onion,* and *behavior.* It also often occurs as part of the sounds represented by the letter *u.*

EXERCISE 228 Pronounce the following words. The letters which represent [j] and a vowel sound are underlined:

Stressed [ju]: union, unit, universe, usual, use, abuse, accuse, amuse, confuse, excuse, refuse, Cuba, cute, acute, future, huge, human, music, musical, numerous, peculiar, pupil, nuisance, beauty, beautiful, few, view, review

Stressed [jʊ]: cure, curious, pure, Europe

Unstressed [ju]: musician

Unstressed [jʊ]: unite, argue, rescue, value, continue, continuous

Unstressed [jə]: argument, calculate, circular, particular, popular, regular, reputation, volume, valuable, onion, union

Unstressed [jɚ]: failure, figure, familiar, peculiar, behavior

EXERCISE 229 Practice the following, applying the principles previously discussed.

1. Her behavior has been peculiar lately.
2. Some views in Europe are really beautiful.
3. The musician refused to continue the performance.
4. He comes from Cuba, doesn't he?
5. The universe is huge.
6. What's the future of the human race?
7. Are onions valuable?
8. Excuse me, please.
9. Pupils are usually curious.
10. Your argument is circular.
11. His music is very popular.
12. A few people confuse me with my brother.
13. Do you think it's a nuisance to have to review?
14. Don't accuse me of taking your book.
15. He has a reputation for being acute.
16. He's familiar with failure.

EXERCISE 230 Review [l] and [r]. Put your tongue tip on your tooth ridge for [l]. Turn your tongue tip upward for [r].

lather — rather	low — row	gloom — groom
leaf — reef	lush — rush	plays — praise
lewd — rude	blight — bright	allay — array
lip — rip	class — crass	file — fire
lock — rock	clutch — crutch	mill — mere
	flute — fruit	

EXERCISE 231 Practice the following, applying the principles previously discussed.

1. I'd rather leave than wait any longer.
2. That was a rude remark.
3. Did your mother rock you when you were a baby?
4. Certain plant diseases are called blights.
5. Don't clutch the baby too tightly, or he'll cry.
6. The children like him because he plays with them.
7. Sometimes I think that man enjoys firing his employees.
8. The ship was wrecked on a reef.
9. Round your lips for that sound.
10. Keep your voices low; don't disturb others.
11. Don't you want to be the best student in the class?
12. Is a tomato a fruit or a vegetable?
13. He's always well groomed, isn't he?
14. He tried to allay her fear by making a joke.
15. She can't do that; she's a mere child.

EXERCISE 232 Review group stress. Stress the noun: lengthen the stressed vowel. Do not stop between the words of a group.

in his face	the burden	of the world
their nests	in my beard	to darkness
the world	like a land	of dreams
for pain	in the middle	of her forehead
the splendor	in story	across the lake
in glory	a crowd	a host
beside the lake	on his back	of the month

EXERCISE 233 Review initial [s] before [t]. Make the [s] with much force. Do not add a vowel before the [s].

still	stop	strange	strict	struggle
stir	storm	stream	strike	student
stock	story	street	string	study
stomach	stove	strength	strip	stuff
stone	straight	stretch	strong	stupid

EXERCISE 234 Practice the following, applying the principles previously discussed.

1. Are you still living on First Street?
2. I wish this storm would stop so I could go to the store.
3. A strong man has a lot of strength.
4. He told us a strange story.
5. That teacher is very strict with his students.
6. I need to stretch; I've been sitting still too long.

LESSON 70 Two-Syllable Words: Stress on Second Syllable

The following words have stress on the second syllable. When you pronounce them, be sure to lengthen the stressed vowel.

1. [i] receive, relief, relieve, repeat, succeed
2. [ɪ] severe, sincere, until, within
3. [e] obey, persuade, relate, remain, replace, today
4. [ɛ] prepare, present (v), pretend, prevent, progress (v), protect, reflect, refresh, regret, request, respect, success, suggest, suspect, unless, yourself
5. [æ] exact, perhaps
6. [ə] result
7. [ɑ] remark, upon, regard
8. [ɔ] inform, perform
9. [o] postpone, propose, suppose
11. [u] refuse (v), review
12. [ɚ] refer, reserve, return
13. [aɪ] remind, reply, resign, retire, supply, surprise, tonight, unite
14. [aʊ] throughout, without
15. [ɔɪ] enjoy, rejoice

146

EXERCISE 235 Practice the following, applying the principles previously discussed.

1. If you don't succeed the first time, try again.
2. Can't I persuade you to have another cup of coffee?
3. What was the result of your interview?
4. Many people hold that author in high regard.
5. Did you reserve a room at the hotel?
6. Do I have to read it throughout?
7. I'll rejoice when he gets fired.
8. That was a severe storm we had last night, wasn't it?
9. Mrs. Lawson, may I present Mr. White?
10. Give me an estimate; the figure doesn't have to be exact.
11. I suppose he did his best.
12. Don't refuse if he asks you for a date.
13. He says he's going to resign from his job.
14. I'll remind you tomorrow.

EXERCISE 236 Review group stress. Stress the noun: lengthen the stressed vowel. Do not stop between the words of a group.

without cooks	for the sink	in beauty
like the night	in her aspect	her eyes
at the start	the night	the day
the light	the time	of shoes
in the forests	of the night	the world

REVIEW: DIALOGS 111-115

111. 1 – What's the hardest thing about English?
     2 – There're a lot of them.
     1 – But what's the hardest?
     2 – The way people speak it.

112. 1 – Most of our worries are caused by our bodies.
     2 – What do you mean by that?
     1 – We get in a bad humor when we're tired or need exercise.
     2 – The Romans knew that.

113. 1 – What does your teacher tell you most often?
     2 – "Practice."
     1 – Is that all he says?
     2 – Well, he says, "Practice correctly."

147

114. 1 – What's the best profession, do you think?
     2 – Engineering.
     1 – I like medicine.
     2 – I suppose the best one's the one you like the most.

115. 1 – It's almost the end of school.
     2 – Yes, I know.
     1 – How many more days are there?
     2 – Six, I think.

REVIEW: QUOTATIONS 64-65

64. There was a little girl
Who had a little curl
Right in the middle of her forehead;
And when she was good,
She was very, very good,
But when she was bad, she was horrid.

                           – Longfellow

65. The splendor falls on castle walls
    And snowy summits old in story;
The long light shakes across the lakes,
    And the wild cataract leaps in glory.
Blow, bugle, blow; set the wild echoes flying;
Blow, bugle; answer, echoes, dying, dying, dying.

                           – Tennyson

LESSON 71   Adjectives Ending in -ed

The following adjectives, which are spelled with the letters *-ed*,
end with unstressed [ɪd]:

hundred	naked	rugged	wicked
kindred	ragged	sacred	wretched

Beloved is usually pronounced [bɪˈləvɪd], sometimes [bɪˈləvd].

148

The following words also have the final -*ed* pronounced [ɪd] when they are used as adjectives:

aged	crooked	jagged
blessed	dogged	learned

Similarly, in compounds with *one-*, *long-*. etc., the word *legged* is pronounced with final [ɪd].

When *aged, blessed,* etc., are used as verbs, the -*ed* is pronounced in accordance with the rules for the past forms of verbs; for instance, *aged* is pronounced [edʒd], and *blessed* is pronounced [blɛst].

EXERCISE 237 Practice the following, applying the principles previously discussed.

1. The aged man talked like a learned scholar.
2. The ragged beggar stared at the jagged rocks.
3. The salesman was dogged in his determination.
4. She gazed at his rugged face with a wicked gleam in her eyes.
5. I think Mrs. Blake has aged considerably since her illness.
6. Bob has grown up to be a long-legged boy.
7. He's learned his lesson.
8. Italian and Spanish are kindred languages.
9. His beloved child had disappeared.
10. We drove along a crooked road.
11. The naked baby looked wretched.
12. The hundred priests prayed to the Blessed Virgin.
13. That soprano sings only sacred songs.
14. A grasshopper is a six-legged creature.
15. The minister blessed the congregation.
16. He slowly crooked his finger at the child.

EXERCISE 238 Review [t] and [d]. Shorten the vowel before [t]; lengthen it before [d]. Don't explode.

bat – bad	eight – aid	hurt – heard
beat – bead	fat – fad	late – laid
bet – bed	fate – fade	mat – mad
boot – booed	hat – had	neat – need
debt – dead	heart – hard	plate – played

EXERCISE 239 Practice the following, applying the principles previously discussed.

1. That's not so bad, is it?
2. When do you go to bed?
3. The crowd booed the umpire.
4. I had to give him first aid.
5. Will this color fade?
6. He has a good heart.
7. He laid it on the seat, didn't he?
8. How many times have you played that record?
9. A bead just dropped off of your necklace.
10. How long has he been dead?
11. Potatoes will make you fat.
12. I didn't do it, but I wish I had.
13. Did it hurt very much?
14. Don't get mad.
15. He has a neat appearance.

EXERCISE 240 Review [ʃ] and [tʃ]. Protrude your lips for [ʃ], but do not stop your breath. Explode the beginning of [tʃ]. Both sounds are voiceless. Make them with force.

share – chair	shin – chin	cash – catch
sheaf – chief	ship – chip	crush – crutch
sheep – cheap	shoe – chew	dish – ditch
sheer – cheer	shoes – choose	lash – latch
sheet – cheat	shop – chop	leash – leech
sheik – cheek	shows – chose	mash – match
she's – cheese		wish – witch

EXERCISE 241 Practice the following, applying the principles previously discussed.

1. Don't take more than your share.
2. Sheep aren't cheap, are they?
3. It's wrong to cheat.
4. She's fond of cheese.
5. Do you want me to chip the ice for the tea?
6. My wife chose that tie.
7. Lame people use crutches.
8. Did you latch the door?
9. Her hat and gloves match, don't they?

150

10. He's the chief of the department.
11. Those stockings are sheer.
12. He kissed her on the cheek.
13. He cut his chin while he was shaving.
14. Puppies like to chew shoes.
15. You should shop around before you buy.
16. I've got to cash a check.
17. He let the water run into the ditch.
18. He bought a leash for his dog.

EXERCISE 242   Review [ts] and [tʃ].   Begin both combinations by putting your tongue tip on your tooth ridge.   Do not protrude your lips for [ts], but protrude them for [tʃ].   Both are voiceless. Make them with much force.

eats — each	eights — h	hunts — hunch
beats — beach	bats — batch	arts — arch
Pete's — peach	cats — catch	starts — starch
pits — pitch	hats — hatch	knots — notch
its — itch	mats — match	watts — watch
wits — witch	pats — patch	coats — coach

EXERCISE 243   Practice the following, applying the principles previously discussed.

1. Each boy eats the same amount.
2. *Pete*'s a short form of *Peter*.
3. Does your back ever itch?
4. Does that word begin with an *h?*
5. They use bats in baseball.
6. How long does it take an egg to hatch?
7. He's got a patch in his pants.
8. That bulb uses forty watts, doesn't it?
9. He's taking his degree in liberal arts.
10. His promotion moved him up another notch.
11. They stayed on the beach all afternoon.
12. Who's going to pitch in the ball game?
13. Keep your wits about you; don't get excited.
14. Did you put the plates on the mats?
15. Cats like to catch mice, don't they?
16. Do you know the story of the hunchback of Notre Dame?
17. Do you want starch in your collars?
18. Her complexion is like peaches and cream.

EXERCISE 244 Review [dz] and [dʒ]. Begin both combinations by putting your tongue tip on your tooth ridge. Do not protrude your lips for [dz], but do protrude them for [dʒ]. Both are voiced. Make them gently.

leads — liege	aids — age	Ed's — edge
seeds — siege	raids — rage	heads — hedge
rids — ridge	wades — wage	buds — budge
	dreads — dredge	

EXERCISE 245 Practice the following, applying the principles previously discussed.

1. People often refer to the siege of Troy.
2. She was scared during the air raids.
3. She's Ed's wife.
4. Almost every student dreads an exam.
5. The buds are beginning to open on those trees.
6. She follows wherever he leads.
7. That powder rids dogs of fleas.
8. What's his age?
9. They have a hedge around their house.
10. That job doesn't pay a living wage.

LESSON 72 Two-Syllable Words: Stress on First Syllable

The following words have stress on the first syllable. When you pronounce them, be sure to lengthen the stressed vowel.

1. [i] meantime, needle, neither, peaceful
2. [ɪ] misery, mixture, mystery, nearly, picture, pity, pretty, prison
3. [e] mainly, maybe, nation, native, nature
4. [ɛ] metal, nephew, never, pencil, penny, pleasant, pleasure, plenty, precious, presence, present (n or adj)
5. [æ] handle, happen, happy, ladder, landlord, language, latter, laughter
6. [ə] number, other, public, punish, puzzle, sunshine, somehow
7. [ɑ] hollow, honest, honor, knowledge, largely, market, model
8. [ɔ] former, fortune, forward, lawyer

152

LESSON 72 (Continued)

9. [o] only, open, over
10. [ʊ] sugar
11. [u] nuisance, numerous
12. [ə] person, purple, purpose, servant
13. [aɪ] likely, private
14. [aʊ] boundary, outline

EXERCISE 246 Practice the following, applying the principles previously discussed.

1. Do you have a needle and thread?
2. What's your native language?
3. You'll have to use a ladder to reach that shelf.
4. The company's just put a new model of that car on the market.
5. When's the class over?
6. Do you like sugar in your coffee?
7. I think he did it on purpose.
8. You should write an outline before you begin your composition.
9. It's a pity she's not pretty, isn't it?
10. My nephew gave me a pencil as a birthday present.
11. Do you like crossword puzzles?
12. Do you think you'd make a fortune if you were a lawyer?
13. It's a nuisance to have the phone ring late at night.
14. It's likely to rain tomorrow.
15. Which metals are precious?
16. It's pleasant to hear happy laughter.

LESSON 73 Words Ending in -ace, -ess, -ice, and -is

A number of words have an unstressed final syllable which contains the letters -ace or -ess or -ice or -is. Those groups of letters are all pronounced alike: [ɪs]. Here are some examples of two-syllable words; the stress is on the first syllable:

furnace	abbess	careless	business	Alice	basis
Horace	actress	endless	darkness	justice	crisis
menace	empress	harmless	illness	malice	Dennis
necklace	goddess	hopeless	kindness	notice	Doris
palace	hostess	reckless	sadness	office	Lois
preface	mattress	thoughtless	sickness	practice	Louis
surface	princess	useless	thickness	service	Paris
terrace	waitress	worthless	witness	Venice	tennis

153

The following three-syllable words have the stress on the first syllable; the ending is pronounced [ɪs]:

bitterness	holiness	loneliness	sinfulness	artifice	prejudice
coziness	liveliness	loveliness	avarice	cowardice	precipice

EXERCISE 247 Practice the following, applying the principles previously discussed.

1. That man's a reckless driver.
2. The princess is wearing her necklace.
3. That waitress will give you good service.
4. Our company has a business office in Paris.
5. Justice has nothing to do with prejudice or malice.
6. Mr. Harris stayed in Venice for a few weeks.
7. The empress stayed in the palace during the crisis.
8. That story was told by the Roman poet Horace, wasn't it?
9. There's a cartoon character called Dennis the Menace.
10. Would you like to eat on the terrace?
11. The boys are going to play tennis, aren't they?
12. You should practice what you preach.
13. Do you like to sleep on a soft mattress?
14. It's useless to argue with me, sir.
15. What was the basis for the judges' decision?
16. The role of the goddess appealed to the actress.
17. Your check was worthless, ma'am.
18. That dog is harmless: he won't bite you.
19. Has Louis got over his illness yet?
20. The hostess polished the surface of the table.
21. Have you read the preface to that book?

EXERCISE 248 Review [f] and [v]. Touch the edges of your upper front teeth lightly with your lower lip. Don't stop your breath. Say [f] with much force. Say [v] with little force. Shorten a stressed vowel before [f]. Lengthen a stressed vowel before [v].

face – vase	rifle – rival	belief – believe
fail – veil	safer – saver	fife – five
fan – van	shuffle – shovel	grief – grieve
fast – vast	infest – invest	half – halve
fat – vat		leaf – leave
fault – vault		proof – prove

EXERCISE 249 Practice the following, applying the principles previously discussed.

1. Do you find fault with movies?
2. Most of their scripts aren't very entertaining, are they?
3. Can you believe many of their plots?
4. You know the story of the waif who grows up to be a thief, don't you?
5. Every lover has to have a rival.
6. Heroes frequently save heroines from drowning in the surf.
7. Nothing is done by half, is it?
8. Fast-moving cars veer just in time.
9. Old men shuffle along, and young men move fast.
10. However, villains always come to grief.
11. Everything finally works out fine.
12. That's life in the movies, isn't it?

EXERCISE 250 Review group stress. Stress the noun: lengthen the stressed vowel. Do not stop between the words of a group.

the rest	a thing	of beauty
the sea	the day	the world
of a number	a world	of things
their melody	the earth	a man
a poem	a tree	in your heart
after school	the mind	his work

EXERCISE 251 Review the -s inflection. Add the sound [ɪz] to the following words:

bless	discuss	march	press
brush	freeze	place	search
dance	manage	practice	seize

EXERCISE 252 Review the -s inflection. Add the sound [s] to the following words:

boast	escape	operate	rip
collect	interrupt	permit	trust
educate	jump	represent	vote

EXERCISE 253   Review the -s inflection.   Add the sound [z] to the following words:

burn	remind	settle	tie
matter	reply	show	weigh
name	roll	struggle	whisper
regard	sail	succeed	wine
relieve	save	suffer	yell
remember	scatter	swallow	zoo

EXERCISE 254   Review [ɚ] and vowel + [r].   Pronounce the following groups.   Turn your tongue tip upward for [ɚ] and [r].

hurt	–	–	heart	–	–
per	peer	pair	par	pour	poor
shirr	sheer	share	–	shore	sure
sir	sear	–	Saar	sore	sewer
stir	steer	stare	star	store	–
were	–	wear	–	war	–
worm	–	–	–	warm	–
–	dear	dare	–	door	–
–	leered	–	lard	lord	lured
–	near	–	–	nor	–
–	sneer	snare	–	snore	–

EXERCISE 255   Practice the following, applying the principles previously discussed.

1. They say smoking hurts your heart.
2. Are you sure we're near the shore?
3. The Saar is frequently a sore spot in politics.
4. I'll be glad when it gets warm again.
5. Lard is made from pork.
6. I wish my roommate didn't snore.
7. The poor man didn't have a pair of shoes, did he?
8. Don't stir until I come back.
9. She wasn't at home, but her parents were.
10. I dare you to open that door.
11. Yes, sir, I'm sure.

156

EXERCISE 256 Review homophones. Pronounce the following pairs alike.

altar – alter	guessed – guest	role – roll
berry – bury	hole – whole	shone – shown
cereal – serial	made – maid	suede – swayed
earn – urn	pain – pane	waist – waste

EXERCISE 257 Practice the following, applying the principles previously discussed.

1. When you die, they bury you.
2. I'm keeping up with a serial in that magazine
3. The whole town's talking about that matter.
4. His greatest role was Othello.
5. Do you like suede shoes?
6. Don't waste your time.
7. I've got a pain in my back.
8. The priest knelt before the altar.
9. How much do you earn?
10. He guessed her secret, didn't he?
11. Do you have a maid?
12. You've broken the window pane.
13. I've shown you how to do this before.
14. She swayed to the music.
15. They put his ashes in an urn.
16. She has a small waist.

EXERCISE 258 Review difference in stress. Pronounce the nouns in the first column with stress on the first syllable. Pronounce the verbs in the second column with stress on the second syllable. Lengthen the stressed vowel.

confine	confine	insert	insert
converse	converse	insult	insult
convict	convict	object	object
extract	extract	permit	permit
frequent (adj)	frequent	produce	produce
increase	increase	progress	progress

157

EXERCISE 259 Practice the following, applying the principles previously discussed.

1. He can converse in three languages.
2. She read an extract from her new novel.
3. You should insert an ad in the paper.
4. He feels you insulted him when you said that.
5. Smoking is not permitted, is it?
6. You should progress from the easy to the difficult.
7. Was he convicted of that crime?
8. He's a frequent visitor at our house.
9. There's been a great increase in population, hasn't there?
10. What's that round object on the other side of the room?
11. They're going to produce that fountain pen in quantities.
12. He's making very good progress.

EXERCISE 260 Review [ɚ] and vowel + [r]. Turn your tongue tip upward when you pronounce [ɚ] and [r].

further	—	farther	—
person	Pearson	parson	—
occurred	—	—	accord
curtain	—	carton	—
—	—	ardor	order

EXERCISE 261 Practice the following, applying the principles previously discussed.

1. Have you heard anything further about the plane crash?
2. Has it ever occurred to you that you might be wrong?
3. Let's get to the show before the curtain goes up.
4. I'm too tired to walk any farther.
5. Mrs. Pearson is the person you'll have to see.
6. I buy cigarets by the carton.
7. His ardor cooled when she told him she was married.
8. The parson hoped the members of his church were in accord with him.

LESSON 74 Two-Syllable Words: Stress on First Syllable

The following words have stress on the first syllable. When you pronounce them, be sure to lengthen the stressed vowel.

1. [i] leader, meaning, meanwhile
2. [ɪ] kitchen, limit, liquid, listen, little, merely, middle, mineral, minute
3. [e] hasten, hasty, lady, lately, lazy
4. [ɛ] lesson, letter, level, many, measure, member, memory, mention, merry, message, treasury
5. [æ] family, fancy, fashion, fasten, gallon, gather, grammar, habit, hammer
6. [ə] Monday, money, monkey, monthly, mother, nothing
7. [ɑ] farther, father, follow, garden, harbor, hardly, harvest
8. [ɔ] daughter, drawer, formal
9. [o] notice, nowhere, ocean
10. [ʊ] purely
11. [u] movement, music
12. [ɚ] merchant, mercy, murder, perfect (adj)
13. [aɪ] kindly, kindness
14. [aʊ] flower

EXERCISE 262 Practice the following, applying the principles previously discussed.

1. He's the leader of the band.
2. Don't be hasty; think it over.
3. He hit his thumb with the hammer.
4. Farmers harvest their crops in the fall.
5. He did it purely by chance.
6. It's been a perfect day.
7. I guess the rose is my favorite flower.
8. I have hardly any money.
9. The cook's in the kitchen.
10. Did you get my message?
11. I'll see your mother on Monday.
12. Have you got a formal notice of your promotion?
13. Do you like Cuban music?
14. He talked to me very kindly.
15. The lady's daughter will be here in a minute.

EXERCISE 263 Review group stress. Stress the noun: lengthen the stressed vowel. Do not stop between the words of a group.

on your head	at your age	a theme
my part	the world	on the sand
of time	a heart	the brain
the eyes	the thing	with feathers
in the soul	without poetry	the tune

EXERCISE 264 Review homophones. Pronounce the following pairs alike.

buy – by	lain – lane	pray – prey
flour – flower	leased – least	son – sun
hall – haul	miner – minor	there – their
higher – hire	one – won	wood – would

EXERCISE 265 Practice the following, applying the principles previously discussed.

1. I've got to buy a bag of flour.
2. He's lain in bed for at least half his life, hasn't he?
3. Some people used to pray to the sun.
4. They're going to hire a hall for the dance.
5. A minor league won the championship.
6. Would you like to go to a movie?

EXERCISE 266 Review [t] and [d]. Shorten the vowel before [t]; lengthen the vowel before [d]. Don't explode.

note – node	set – said	sweet – Swede
rate – raid	sight – side	threat – thread
root – rude	slight – slide	trait – trade
rot – rod	spite – spied	wait – weighed
sat – sad	state – stayed	write – ride
seat – seed	suit – sued	wrote – rode

160

EXERCISE 267 Practice the following, applying the principles previously discussed.

1. I'll make a note about the appointment.
2. The tooth had an abcess on the root.
3. Cheer Sarah up; she looks sad.
4. Do you know what he said?
5. We're trying to win him over to our side.
6. Isn't that a new suit you have on?
7. The baby-sitter stayed until the parents got home.
8. He's got all his father's bad traits.
9. They rode all the way home without saying a word.
10. Let's make a raid on the icebox.
11. He's buying a new fishing rod.
12. He planted a seed of suspicion in her mind.
13. Oh, it's only a slight headache.
14. In spite of what I told you, you didn't do it.
15. We have two Swedes in our class.
16. He says that country is a threat to peace.
17. Why didn't you wait until I got there?
18. Did you write your composition then?

REVIEW: DIALOGS 116-120

116. 1 — The weather isn't nice today, is it?
     2 — No, it certainly isn't.
     1 — It's too humid.
     2 — Yes, that's the trouble.

117. 1 — Have you ever been stung by a bee?
     2 — Yes, I have.
        When I was very young.
     1 — What happened?
     2 — I fainted.

118. 1 — I didn't get any mail this morning.
     2 — That's too bad.
     1 — I'm worried about my family
     2 — Oh, well, you know, no news is good news.

119. 1 – I'm sorry I'm late.
      2 – That's all right.
           What happened?
      1 – Traffic got held up by an accident.
      2 – Was anybody hurt?
      1 – No, fortunately.

120. 1 – Today's the last day of school.
      2 – Yes, it is.
      1 – Aren't you glad?
      2 – I don't know.

REVIEW: QUOTATIONS 66-67

66. I wandered lonely as a cloud
     That floats on high o'er vales and hills,
     When all at once I saw a crowd,
     A host, of golden daffodils,
     Beside the lake, beneath the trees,
     Fluttering and dancing in the breeze.

                            — *Wordsworth*

67. Yet each man kills the thing he loves;
     By each let this be heard.
     Some do it with a bitter look;
     Some with a flattering word.
     The coward does it with a kiss;
     The brave man with a sword.

                            — *Wilde*

INDEX